MW01054074

ELK HUNTING
MONTANA

ELK HUNTING
MONTANA

FINDING SUCCESS ON THE BEST PUBLIC LANDS

Jack Ballard

The Lyons Press
Guilford, Connecticut
An imprint of The Globe Pequot Press

To buy books in quantity for corporate use
or incentives, call **(800) 962–0973,**
or e-mail **premiums@GlobePequot.com.**

Copyright © 2008 Jack Ballard

ALL RIGHTS RESERVED. No part of this book may be reproduced or transmitted in any form by any means, electronic or mechanical, including photocopying and recording, or by any information storage and retrieval system, except as may be expressly permitted in writing from the publisher. Requests for permission should be addressed to The Lyons Press, Attn: Rights and Permissions Department, P.O. Box 480, Guilford, CT 06437.

The Lyons Press is an imprint of The Globe Pequot Press.

10 9 8 7 6 5 4 3 2 1

Printed in the United Sates of America

Designed by Carol Sawyer/Rose Design

ISBN 978-1-59921-154-1

Library of Congress Cataloging-in-Publication Data is available on file.

This book is dedicated to all individuals and organizations who strive to improve Montana's elk habitat, preserve backcountry areas from roads and development, and secure access to public land for the common citizen.

CONTENTS

------------◆------------

ACKNOWLEDGMENTS

----------◆----------

Many people besides the author contributed to the creation of this book. From Forest Service personnel who produce maps to dedicated Montana Dept. of Fish, Wildlife & Parks folks who run big-game check stations, the information compiled and produced by total strangers has been essential to my writing. I've also relied upon the generous sharing of knowledge by relatives, friends, and fellow hunters from across Montana.

This book would not have been published (at least not on the publisher's time-line) without the many hours my wife, Fran, spent revising the text and creating time for me to write.

Finally, I am infinitely indebted to the Creator of the eternal blue sky whose breath stirs life in all things, wild and human. May we respect the earth and one another as His handiwork.

INTRODUCTION

---------------◆---------------

When I set out to write this book, I felt I had a pretty good handle on the Montana elk-hunting scene. Except for a brief stint in Kentucky for education, I've lived my entire life in the state and hunted elk since I could convince Dad to drag me with him to the mountains. Along the way, I've hunted wapiti from a backpacker's camp in the Absaroka-Beartooth Wilderness, skulked in the timber above Buffalo Horn Creek in the Gallatin Range, waited for daylight at the edge of Poe Park in the Elkhorns, pointed a horse into the Babcock Creek drainage of the Bob Marshall Wilderness, and hunted the West Fork of the Ruby River enough to navigate my way around by starlight—not to mention other elk forays into the Madison Range, the Bitterroot Mountains, and the East Custer country south of Ashland.

Nonetheless, the scope and scale of elk habitat in the Treasure State and its wealth of public land has reminded me how little I've actually seen. One could literally hunt a lifetime of seasons and cover but a small fraction of Montana's *Cervus elaphus* country. Consequently, I offer this book not as a compendium of areas I've hunted but more of a researched overview of places where you might find me should we happen to choose the same mountain range or swatch of habitat next fall. Though tedious and mentally exhausting, the research required to produce this book has bestowed many unexpected rewards, not the least of which are three specific destinations I'm impassioned to hunt next season (and yes, they are also described for *you* in the text).

Along with increasing my knowledge of elk hunting in Montana, this project has reminded me how blessed I am to live in a state with such a wealth of public land resources and how important it is to conserve them if my children are to enjoy similar opportunities. When you close the book, I hope you feel the same.

HOW TO USE THIS BOOK

-----------◆-----------

If you've never bought a book with an owner's manual, here's the first. Take a few minutes to read this section, as it will help make sense of some of the terminology herein and assist in interpreting data in the tables.

Although the book doesn't cover every elk-hunting destination in Montana, it comes pretty close. However, more words are devoted to the regions that hold the greatest appeal to hunters because of the number of elk they harbor, their reputation for trophy animals, or their unique settings for a hunt.

To condense the text, I've used a number of abbreviations. *MDFWP* refers to the Montana Dept. of Fish, Wildlife & Parks. *HD* stands for hunting district, *NF* for national forest. *WMA* means wildlife management area, and *NWR* means national wildlife refuge. *BLM* is a standard abbreviation for Bureau of Land Management. *BMA* stands for block management area, an area of private land open to regulated public hunting.

Undoubtedly, you'll want to pair this reference with maps as you plan your hunting. DeLorme's big *Montana Atlas & Gazetteer* goes with me nearly everywhere I hunt. The U.S. Forest Service continues to improve its maps, now offering tear-resistant versions with travel information for nearly every national forest in the state. These are the two primary references I've relied upon in providing directions to the various areas identified in this book and for names or numbers of roads.

However, I realize that names on maps don't always square with signs on the roads, if they're even there in the first place. Therefore, I've given multiple titles for many routes, such as Fish Creek Road (FR 343), along with a geographic reference (runs along Fish Creek) so that you can find your way to an area even if routes are poorly marked in the field. The abbreviation *FR* generally refers to routes with some portion maintained by federal agencies (BLM or Forest Service). *RD* describes county or other roads. The first mention of a highway includes its designation as a state or U.S. route; subsequent references do not. Additionally, I've provided estimates—rough estimates—of driving distances when I thought they'd be helpful.

For people traveling from other parts of the country, let me also point out that "road" is a relative term. You should find most of the main routes I've described easily passable with a pickup, and some can be driven in a passenger car, should you wish to hunt from your family station wagon. However, you may occasionally find roads that branch from these choked with boulders, steep enough to frighten a mountain goat, or pinched through sharp-needled pines that compete for paint scratches on four-wheel drives. Just because a route is technically open to motorized vehicle travel doesn't mean you'll actually want to drive it.

One final note regarding travel: Remember that resource management on public lands is an ongoing process. Some of the roads and trails I've described may one day be closed or managed with different travel restrictions. If you encounter this situation, don't panic. With a little map-work and scouting, you can probably find an alternate route or a nearby drainage to hunt.

Along with "how to get there" resources, this book contains information about what to expect in terms of elk populations and whereabouts once you arrive. In each chapter I've described general or specific locations of elk winter range. During the archery and early weeks of the general season, expect to find animals at higher elevations, sometimes a considerable distance from wintering grounds. Toward the end of the general season, they're often found in locations adjacent to winter range. Sometimes animals don't arrive at their normal wintering grounds until after the general elk season, though most years will find them heading in that direction beforehand. Every regional chapter also contains a number of charts rating specific mountain ranges or other areas in relation to various attributes: elk numbers, hunters per square mile, hunters per elk, trophy potential, and remote or roadless areas. Here's how to understand them:

Each of the ratings compares the location it describes with other areas in Montana. For *elk numbers, hunters per square mile,* and *hunters per elk,* I used current statistics and historical trends from MDFWP data to determine the highest and lowest figures in the state, then divided them into four equal segments: low, moderate, high, and very high. The *trophy potential* rating is primarily based on MDFWP harvest data, but anecdotal evidence from other veteran hunters and personal experience also factor into this measure, which represents a hunter's chance of killing a bull with six points on at least one antler. However, "very high" doesn't imply that a big bull waits behind every pine but that, in relation to other destinations, the described unit offers some of the best odds of producing a trophy. For the *remote/roadless* areas rating, "low" refers to those areas where it's difficult to find much territory a mile beyond a road. The "very high" end includes those dominated by large, designated wilderness areas closed to wheeled-vehicle travel of any kind. I believe these tables will be a very helpful reference, but keep in mind that local conditions sometimes vary from the norm. Tramp the backcountry in an area of high hunter densities, and you may not spy another human. Find the best habitat in a region of low elk numbers, and you might stumble into multiple herds. The tables cover the general rules but don't apply to the exceptions.

1

WHEN TO HUNT

-------------◆-------------

Montana hunters are blessed with some of the finest opportunities for elk stalking anywhere in the nation. The state's sprawling geography, excellent habitat, and high elk numbers certainly make it one of the top destinations in the West. However, one aspect of elk hunting in Big Sky Country that truly sets it apart is the duration of its seasons.

While most states offer elk hunting for just a few weeks—or days—each year, Montana's general elk seasons typically run from early September to late November. Archery season opens around Labor Day weekend and extends through mid-October. The general season that opens the woods to rifle wielders historically begins the fourth Sunday in October and ends the Sunday after Thanksgiving. Special seasons for particular game-management objectives may be available before, concurrent with, or after the general season. As elk dispersion and behavior varies markedly from early to late autumn, knowledge of the life cycle during that time will greatly enhance your hunting. Local and seasonal variations occur, but here's the general pattern in Montana.

Prelude to the Rut

In most places the first to get a whack at the year's elk crop are bowhunters. Archery season opens around the first of September, although many archers wait for two or three weeks before seriously hitting the field.

What are bulls doing at this time of year? Mature animals have recently rubbed the velvet from their antlers, and bachelor herds that grazed placidly together just weeks before have splintered. Lone, wandering males are now the norm, bugling occasionally and polishing their headgear but not actively seeking to gather a harem.

While many bowhunters avoid the early days of the elk season altogether because of the heat and lack of rutting activity, there are actually some positives during this time period. The number one advantage is that bulls will likely be on their own, not surrounded by a gaggle of twenty sharp-eyed cows. True, they may not yet respond to a bugle or cow call, but their own infrequent bugles may be enough to let you pinpoint the exact location of a lone bull and sneak within arrow range.

Phases of the Rut

Within a couple of weeks of this staging period, breeding-age bulls move into the cow herds. One September I spied a tremendous, solitary bull on a Labor Day outing. A week later, right at the tenth of the month, he imposed his company on a large herd of cows in a nearby valley.

By the third week in September, the rut is in full swing. Dominant bulls have claimed their harems. Spikes and other stags short on bulk and antler are driven from the cow herds by the great harem masters. During this time bulls tending cows bugle boisterously, often accompanying their vocal barrage with the destruction of some hapless sapling or the rapacious raking of a larger tree. While bulls may be relatively easy to find during the height of the breeding season, they can be maddeningly difficult to hunt—especially for bowhunters. As often as not, the stag is occupied at the center of a vigilant herd of cows and their young. Get past eight pairs of eyes, and the nose of the ninth female will send the herd crashing into the lodgepoles. Nonetheless, most archers prefer hunting the height of the rut for its excitement and because previously edgy bulls may now be hopelessly distracted by a harem.

Under the right circumstances, though, you might score big without even dealing with a herd bull. As is the case with other species, *Cervus elaphus* males that are the biggest in antler and body aren't necessarily the most aggressive. Each fall I photograph rutting elk in Yellowstone

A bull's bugling during the rut makes it easier to find, an advantage most enjoyed by bowhunters.

National Park. On numerous occasions I've spotted tremendous bulls that haven't gathered a harem and don't appear anxious to acquire one. My older brother, Leroy, once arrowed a huge nontypical with seventeen antler points that was completely alone, though the rut was in overdrive.

In a handful of backcountry hunting districts, rifle-toting hunters can challenge bugling bulls along with the archers. These early rifle seasons occur in the Absaroka-Beartooth Wilderness north of Yellowstone National Park and in the Bob Marshall Wilderness south of Glacier National Park.

Somewhere around the first of October, most breeding-age cows have conceived next year's calf and no longer come into heat. However, the mating fever is still hot upon the bulls, making them intensely competitive to find late-cycling females or those who didn't conceive a calf on the first mating. In my thinking this is the best phase of the breeding cycle for targeting brutish bulls with bugling and cow calls. During this time both herd bulls and wandering males seem much more inclined to investigate vocal indications of other elk. Some very large bulls are taken each year at the tail end of the rut. If an archer can't hunt earlier, there's still action aplenty toward the end of the breeding season.

After the Rut

As rutting activity winds down in mid- to late October, the general elk season opens. Some bulls are still tending herds, but a curious thing often happens. A month before, a single, dominant bull usually held his harem against all rivals. Now, however, there may be several breeding-age bulls intermingled with a large herd of cows. On our family ranch, I once observed a herd of nearly a hundred elk during this period—a dozen of which were branch-antlered bulls. The same phenomenon also occurs on public land. A season or two ago, a friend and I watched a band of animals on the eve of the season opener in late October. Of the thirty or so elk, seven of them were bulls who had long since shed their spikes.

They've lost weight during the rut, so older bulls must gain weight for the winter. They're easier to find and stalk when feeding.

Large bands with multiple bulls form a sizeable chunk of the elk population at this time, a phenomenon that also occurs in some places at the peak of the rut, but one thing changes the herd composition in a hurry—human hunters. In areas where opening day signals a swarm of orange-clad riflemen roaming the mountains, the big bands of elk rapidly splinter into smaller groups. Most mature bulls that haven't already done so quickly forsake the cows altogether.

After hunting pressure or the natural life cycle nudges bulls away from the cows, look for solitary stags in secure habitat. Having lost an incredible amount of weight during the rut—sometimes in excess of two hundred pounds—dominant bulls retreat to strongholds where they can eat, rest, and restore body condition for the coming winter.

Timbered, north-facing slopes are favored haunts of these post-rut bulls. One fall I helped two novice hunters down the first bragging-size elk of their hunting careers. Both six-points were found on a huge, north-facing incline interspersed with tiny clearings. Every year I find lone bulls holed up on this slope. And why not? There's plenty to eat in the grassy openings, numerous rivulets to provide water, and a secure place to nap away the daylight hours undisturbed by all but a few hunters.

Staging for Winter

Somewhere around the middle of November, bulls that two months before tried to disembowel one another with pointed weapons of war once again become bosom buddies. From now until next August, when the bachelor bands break up prior to the rut, mature males are most often found in one another's company, passing the winter in groups of just a few or as many as a couple of dozen animals.

In terms of habitat, bulls trying to bulk up for the winter look for two things: plenty to eat and an undisturbed place to rest. Remote areas with secure bedding cover and abundant forage are excellent places to find big bulls at this stage of the season. Timbered areas interspersed with small meadows often attract bachelor herds; they feed in the clearings, then retreat to the evergreens to bed.

Because they need to regain weight lost during the rut, lean males spend a good part of their day feeding, nibbling grass and other palatable plants in the security of the timber. They also tend to drift into the meadows or other foraging areas earlier in the evening and hang there later in the morning.

Another phenomenon of the elk cycle that often occurs in the latter days of November is the migration. Not all herds of elk are migratory, nor do migrations occur at the same time every year. However, when they do happen, the seasonal treks of wapiti from the high country to lower wintering grounds often put them in accessible areas that only days before may have held but a handful of resident elk.

What triggers a migration? "It's a combination of factors," a noted biologist once told me. "If you get significant snowfall, elk will move. But temperature also has an effect. In some places elk migrate even without heavy snow or cold."

Like cows, mature bulls also migrate. But they typically move a bit later and winter at higher elevations. Research reported by the Wildlife Management Institute indicates that bulls are more tolerant of deep snow. The same body of data also shows that they tend to inhabit slightly higher altitudes than cows and calves throughout the winter. Thus, at migration time, hunters searching for the oldest, largest males are well advised to target open ridges and south-facing slopes above the female herds.

The *Cervus elaphus* life cycle that I've described characterizes the typical pattern of elk behavior in Montana. However, local variations to "normal" behaviors and rhythms do occur. Increasing your knowledge of the elk's life cycle and biology probably won't land you a weekend job as a wildlife biologist. But maybe that's just as well. Put your knowledge of the autumn patterns to use hunting, and you'll need your spare time for other things—like butchering elk.

2

HOW TO HUNT

------------◆------------

This book is primarily a reference for where to hunt elk in Montana, but regardless of what area you target, your success also depends on your hunting strategies. In this chapter I'll outline some of the most basic and productive tactics for dropping a Big Sky bull—or cow, for that matter. Consistently successful elk hunters share two common attributes: They're intimately familiar with the country they hunt, and they routinely adapt their strategies to current conditions. Once you've chosen an area, stick with it for a few seasons. At my family's camp in the southwestern corner of the state, we usually double or triple the overall hunter-success rate. I'd like to think we're extraordinary hunters, but probably the greatest factor underlying our success is more than fifty years' history hunting the same area. If you choose a productive area and scour it persistently for a few seasons, you should get to the point where you expect to find an elk every year—providing you adopt fruitful hunting strategies. Here are some of the best.

The Artful Ambush

Is there any predictability to the movements of an animal whose home range encompasses several square miles? While the logical answer seems to be no, reality proves otherwise, at least in relation to elk. Wapiti can be "patterned" and ambushed under a variety of conditions.

Careful glassing can reveal awesome ambush possibilities on opening morning.

In arid environments or drought years, intercept elk en route to water sources. The big critters need more fluid than smaller mammals and often return to the same drinking hole every day. This tactic is especially effective for archery hunters, as archery season occurs early, when water sources may be limited and temperatures are high enough to keep elk thirsty.

However, ambushes aren't only effective around water. For decades members of my family have blindsided bulls crossing open ridges during the first days of the general season. Hunting pressure from below pushes them over the top, where my cold-tolerant cousins huddle in rock piles at ten thousand feet. Ambushes of this variety demand some history with an area, as it takes several years to determine how pressure moves local elk. Once their travel routes are determined, this strategy works year after year.

The onset of the rifle season often brings ambush opportunities in other locations. Undisturbed by humans, wapiti often feed on the same meadow or the same hillside for an extended period of time. If possible, I like to arrive at my hunting destination a few days before the season opens. I glass likely areas at daylight and dusk, searching for a herd or a particular animal I'll target on opening morning. This often means hiking for a couple of hours in the dark just prior to the season's opening bell, but this tactic is very successful. Nearly every season I have shooting opportunities at first light by closing in on elk I've patterned for ambush in the previous days.

Stealthy Still-Hunting

Poorly suited for individuals with low frustration tolerance, still-hunting is, I think, the tactic most widely used by master elk hunters during rifle seasons in traditional mountain habitat. Here's why. Hunting pressure quickly drives wapiti into the timber on opening day. There they stay, often coming out only at night to feed. As the average elk hunter has only average frustration tolerance, he stays out of the timber because his store of expletives is insufficient for the number of times he's outwitted.

But get this: If you're outsmarted seven out of eight times still-hunting, that still puts you in elk steak if you stay with it. Sneaking around in the timber obviously works best when the ground is damp, keeping foot noise to a minimum. However, windy days also make for fruitful still-hunting, even when it's bone dry. Creaking trees and air rushing through pine needles effectively muffle footfalls, even on dry twigs.

Although I don't still-hunt with my back to the breeze, I'm not terribly fussy about determining wind direction, as it often changes in the timber. Instead, I search for areas where I expect to find elk and then move in as the wind dictates. Even in a two-thousand-acre expanse of timber that is uniform in species and density, elk have their preferred haunts. From mid-morning to late afternoon, you'll most often find them bedded on level benches or resting on the crests of bulges and ridgelines.

This tactic works any time during the fall, but it seems especially productive for late-season bulls. As I've said before, lean males need to regain the weight they lost during the rut, so they spend a good part of their day feeding, mostly in the security of the timber, though they do drift into the open early in the evening and later in the morning.

The fact that bulls are on their feet more during this time tips the hand in favor of the skilled still-hunter. Once, while easing slowly through the timber, a friend of mine killed an excellent bull that I spotted less than a hundred yards ahead of us. Even though it was nearly noon,

Still-hunting is an excellent elk-hunting technique, but requires patience aplenty.

the hungry stag was on his feet, feeding, when I glimpsed his head rising from the tiny shrubs he was browsing. Had the bull been bedded, it's likely he would have scored first in the spotting game. Standing or moving elk are much easier to see than those lying on the forest floor. Sneaking in the timber is a good strategy nearly any time you're hunting elk, but it's doubly effective in the weeks before the onset of winter.

Effective still-hunting requires stealth and patience. Move very slowly. If you spot one elk, spend time looking for more—they're usually not alone. But you probably will be. Although it's a proven tactic, few have the stomach for still-hunting.

Terrific Tracking

To this elk hunter's eye, there's no finer sight than waking to a tent covered in white. Finding, following, and stalking wapiti are all easier with snow. Elk are more active after a storm and easier to see. You can't plan a hunt around a snowstorm, but if it happens, put all your energy into exploiting the results.

After a storm I move quickly, looking for tracks. If hunting only bulls, this means locating a single, large print or a small band of adult animals, which often indicates a bachelor herd. Once on promising tracks, I follow at a brisk pace until activity—meandering, feeding, etc.—indicates that I'm closing in or they're preparing to bed. At that point I slow to the proverbial snail's crawl and essentially quit trailing and start still-hunting in the direction of the tracks. How effective is tracking? One season I trailed within shooting distance of five bulls in three different bands in a single day.

Designer Drives

The age-old tactic of "driving" whitetail deer can also be successfully adapted to elk hunting—if it's used in the right habitats. As mentioned earlier, elk tend to hole up within days or hours of encountering hunters in the fall. In many mountain ranges this means they flee to patches of timber or move into the dark haunts of thickly forested north-facing slopes.

To push elk from isolated patches of timber, locate a shooter on a vantage point with excellent visibility and a solid rest, downwind of the direction you expect elk to exit the timber. Other members of the party should then move through the area from which you're intending to flush animals, being alert for possible shooting opportunities but moving at a brisk pace. If a particular chunk of cover doesn't yield elk, switch shooters and drivers, then try again elsewhere.

Successfully driving large expanses of elk cover is more difficult. Unlike whitetails, who often develop favorite escape routes from hiding areas, elk may run from the same bedding area one day but bust out in an opposite direction the next. However, on timbered slopes that lie beneath drainage divides, elk can sometimes be pushed to waiting hunters above timberline. If you're on a ridgeline with thick timber below, it's possible to conduct a drive by leaving a shooter in place and then sending one or more drivers through the timber in a route that resembles a large loop. Ideally, the driver or drivers should head into the timber a couple of hundred yards up or down ridge from the shooter. The driver should then work into the timber for another couple of hundred yards and then turn and come back upslope toward the shooter. This technique is tough on the poor guy that has to make the drive back up a steep slope, but I've seen it work on a number of occasions. Perhaps the key is recruiting tough, young hunting partners and channeling their enthusiasm to one's own benefit!

Productive habitat, proven tactics, and patience are all it takes to win at "do it yourself" elk hunting on Montana's public lands. Isn't it time you joined the game?

3

WHERE TO HUNT

---------------◆---------------

You can drop several thousand dollars on an outfitted elk hunt. The investment might afford an opportunity at a trophy bull, but someone else (your guide) does the hunting. You're pretty much there just to pull the trigger.

Wouldn't it be more satisfying to do it all on your own—from choosing an area to hunt to matching wits one-on-one with a wapiti? For any competent big-game hunter, a "do it yourself" elk kill on public land is a reasonable goal and not as difficult as one might imagine. In Montana literally millions of acres of public land beckon the elk hunter. Here's an overview of the options.

National Forests

Federally managed national forests compose the largest portion of public land open to elk hunters. Sketch a line on your state map from Glacier National Park in the northwest to Yellowstone National Park in the southwest. Scan the map west of that line, and a quick analysis shows more national forest land in the western portion of the state than private land. National forests in this area host most of the state's elk hunters, for good reason. There are plenty of elk, virtually unlimited opportunities, and destinations ideal for nearly any hunting ability and style.

Although national forests are typically open to hunting without restrictions, travel is another matter. Portions of federal land are sometimes closed to vehicle

The author and an assistant (Molly) with a big Montana bull from the Beaverhead National Forest.

travel and may have seasonal closures regulating the types of vehicles that can be used in specific areas. Before you finalize your hunting plans to a national forest, familiarize yourself with its travel regulations.

Almost without exception, the best elk hunting is found furthest from motorized-vehicle access. Designated wilderness areas and regions that prohibit motorized travel may be harder to reach but typically hold more elk and a higher percentage of older bulls for those whose hunting is as much about antlers as a freezer filled with meat. In my mind that's about as compelling a reason for hunters to support roadless land management as there is, but we'll save that discussion for another time.

Many hunters pitch elk camps on national forest lands, but if you're planning to camp, do your homework. In some areas most national forest campgrounds close before the general elk season opens, although many may be available during bow season. A quick call to the appropriate office is all it takes to determine whether the campground you've chosen remains open during hunting season. Alternately, it's usually legal to pitch a camp on national forest lands for ten days or more, provided there aren't area-specific regulations regarding campsites. Again, contacting the management office of a particular unit of the national forest will secure the necessary information, which sometimes is also available on the Internet.

Archers and other early-season elk hunters who plan to target national forests also need to check for land-use restrictions connected to fire activity. September often spells significant wildfire activity in Montana. In some cases federal lands may be completely closed to public use during periods of fire activity or drought conditions. I personally know of a nonresident hunter who made a long pilgrimage to hunt a wilderness area in September; only on his arrival did he learn that the area was closed. Luckily for him, the fire restrictions were lifted two days later. Had they remained in effect, his time and travel money would have been wasted.

In much of western Montana, particularly the Absaroka-Beartooth Wilderness, the Bob Marshall Wilderness, areas adjacent to Yellowstone National Park, and vicinities surrounding these locations, elk hunters share public lands with black and grizzly bears. Consequently, extra caution must be taken regarding camping, food storage, and game retrieval. If you're not knowledgeable about recreating in bear country, an excellent resource is Bill Schneider's book, *Bear Aware*. This pocket-size guide covers all the information you need to camp and hunt safely with grizzly neighbors.

Bureau of Land Management (BLM) Lands

For the most part elk hunting on BLM lands occurs in the eastern half of the state. The most notable area is the Missouri Breaks, which sprawl around Fort Peck Reservoir and the Missouri River. Elsewhere, elk are found on scattered tracts of BLM ground in the extreme southeastern portion of the state and along the Tongue and Powder river breaks near the Wyoming border. Significant parcels of BLM land also dot the landscape in the foothills and mountains of southwestern Montana.

In general, the rules of access and travel on BLM lands are similar to those governing national forests. Motorized travel is restricted to established routes, unless otherwise posted. Sadly, some hunters routinely ignore these regulations, driving cross-country or into areas that are closed

Young bulls spar on public ground in the foothills. Most BLM land is found in foothills and prairie locations.

to vehicle travel. Don't align yourself with these lawbreakers. Road closures on BLM lands maintain habitat security for wildlife, elk included, and help to curb the spread of noxious weeds, one of the greatest threats to habitat on Montana's public lands. If you want to hunt vehicle-restricted areas on BLM land, muster the gumption to hike, horseback, or pedal a mountain bike.

Few developed campgrounds exist on BLM land, but camping is generally allowed anywhere, except in those areas (which are very few) where regulations prohibit overnight occupation. Otherwise, camping is allowed anywhere it doesn't interfere with other authorized activities such as timber sales or oil development. Campfires can usually be built without restriction, but as with other federal lands, BLM acreages may be closed to open fires during times of elevated wildfire risk. Another general camping rule involves the maximum duration of stay, which is fourteen days, unless a local BLM office has instituted other camping regulations.

Other Federal Lands

Elk hunting is found on some units of the national wildlife refuge (NWR) system and may be available on land administered by the Bureau of Reclamation as well. The Charles M. Russell NWR north of the Missouri River is one example of such property.

Without exception, check directly with local management offices of these areas before hunting. National wildlife refuges often provide public hunting but may have specific regulations concerning species, seasons, and what portions of the refuge are open to hunting.

State Lands

Perhaps one shouldn't be overly critical of one's home state, but Montana bureaucrats seem especially adept at endlessly tweaking the laws concerning public access to state lands. The good news is, however, that nearly all state lands are open to hunting, and some of them offer excellent opportunities for elk.

Land-use regulations on state lands are typically a little more restrictive than on federal lands. For example, camping outside developed campgrounds is currently limited to two nights and is allowed only within two hundred feet of a legal-access point. Open fires are prohibited, and motorized travel is restricted to designated routes.

In some areas state lands comprise both game preserves and wildlife management areas (WMAs). Game preserves are generally closed to hunting. WMAs usually allow hunting, although specific rules may apply. In short, it's imperative to determine the status and regulations of any state lands you think you might utilize while elk hunting.

Block Management Areas

Block management areas (BMAs) are not public land but do provide for public hunting. The block management program relies on the cooperation of private landowners, in conjunction with the Montana Dept. of Fish, Wildlife & Parks to provide hunting.

Here's how it works. Private landowners voluntarily open their properties to public hunting, for which they are paid a fee. Individual landowners still maintain all private-property rights and control of their land, even when enrolled in the program.

Plum Creek Timber

In western Montana Plum Creek Timber, Inc. (PCT) owns and manages millions of acres for forest production. The company has a long-standing policy of allowing public use of its holdings, including access for hunting. As part of its management policies, logging roads on PCT properties are often closed to motorized travel.

Illegal use of these routes by ATVs for hunting and game retrieval is a growing problem. In the strongest possible terms, let me remind you that hunters on PCT acres are guests of the corporation. Respect the rules, and make it a point to say, "Thank you."

A list of BMAs in each administrative region of the MDFWP is currently available on August 15. The program annually enrolls literally millions of acres, with numerous properties open to elk hunting in nearly every region. However, each BMA has its own set of rules regarding access and hunting restrictions. Some BMAs allow motorized access on specific roads, while others are open to foot and horse travel only. Certain BMAs allow hunters to simply sign in at a self-administered check-in site. Others require advance permission from the landowner. It is the *hunter's* responsibility to be aware of—and comply with—the specific rules for each BMA.

Elk hunters find good hunting on BMAs, though access to this species isn't as prevalent as opportunities to hunt deer and antelope. Except in limited-entry elk units, BMAs likely won't produce many large bulls but are often an excellent option for hunters with antlerless tags.

Key Contacts for Public Land Information

National Forests

Northern Region Headquarters, Federal Building, 200 E. Broadway, Missoula, MT 59807 (406-329-3551); *www.fs.fed.us/r1*

Beaverhead-Deerlodge National Forest, 420 Barrett St., Dillon, MT 59725 (406-683-3900)

Bitterroot National Forest, 1801 N. 1st St., Hamilton, MT 59840 (406-363-7100)

Custer National Forest, 1310 Main St., Billings, MT 59105 (406-657-6200)

Flathead National Forest, 1935 Third Ave. E., Kalispell, MT 59901 (406-758-5204)

Gallatin National Forest, Federal Building, 10 E. Babcock, Bozeman, MT 59771 (406-587-6701)

Helena National Forest, 2880 Skyway Dr., Helena, MT 59602 (406-449-5201)

Kootenai National Forest, 1101 U.S. Highway 2 West, Libby, MT 59923 (406-293-6211)

Lewis and Clark National Forest, 1101 15th St. N., Great Falls, MT 59405 (406-791-7700)

Lolo National Forest, Fort Missoula-Building 24, Missoula, MT 59804 (406-329-3750)

Bureau of Land Management

Montana State Office, 5001 Southgate Dr., Billings, MT 59107 (406-896-5000)

State Lands

Montana Department of Natural Resources & Conservation, 1625 Eleventh Ave., Helena, MT 59620 (406-444-2074)

Block Management Areas

Montana Dept. of Fish, Wildlife & Parks, 1420 East 6th Ave., Helena, MT 59620 (406-444-2535)

Plum Creek Timber

140 North Russell, Missoula, MT 59801 (406-728-8350)

4

NORTHEAST,
EASTERN MISSOURI BREAKS

------------◆------------

Geographical Overview

When Lewis and Clark forged through what is now northeastern Montana on their historic trek up the Missouri River more than two centuries ago, they greeted a prairie landscape teeming with wildlife: bison, wolves, antelope, grouse, grizzly bears . . . and elk. Less than a century after the Corps of Discovery surveyed the area, the three largest indigenous mammals were extirpated by sharp-eyed hunters and hungry sod busters. Gone were the huge, clawed prints of grizzly tracks on sandbars along the winding Missouri. Gone were the huffing herds of hairy bison galloping across the prairie. Silenced were the bugles of lusty bull elk that echoed in the coulees and badlands along the mighty river.

Although winters in this eastern segment of Montana's "High Line" are severe, ample snowfall and summer rains sprout plenty of forage for grazing animals and nourish exceptional antlers on the elk that once again track this historic area. While much of this country is relatively flat, deep coulees, jagged hills, and hideously contorted breaks fan from the Missouri River drainage, sprinkled with junipers and surprisingly dense patches of ponderosa pines.

At Fort Peck a massive earthen dam contains the Missouri River in the Fort Peck Reservoir. This lake extends more than one hundred miles up the river. The UL Bend Wilderness and the Charles M. Russell NWR extend from the shores of

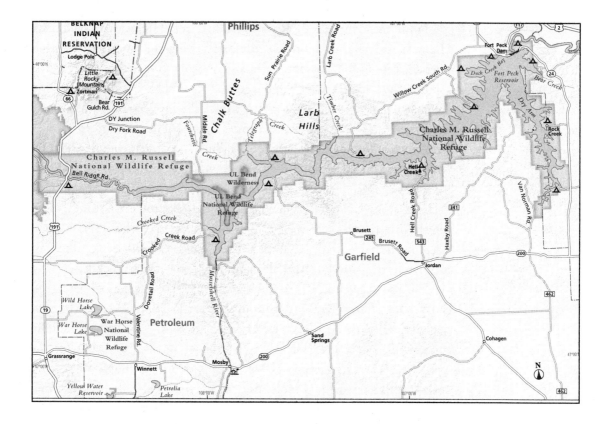

the lake, sustaining natural habitat for a host of wildlife species, including elk that have repopulated much of their native range throughout the ridges and ravines along the river, a segment of country commonly known as the Missouri Breaks.

Elk Distribution

East of the Dry Arm of Fort Peck Lake and south of the Missouri River, elk are scattered among the hills, mainly in areas isolated from vehicle travel and offering security in the form of rough terrain and timber. South of the lake, wapiti range throughout the timbered breaks along some eighty miles from the Dry Arm westward to the Musselshell River. Compared to other portions of the Missouri Breaks, elk numbers are fairly low in this region.

From the Musselshell River west to State Highway 19 and U.S. Highway 191, elk are more plentiful, occupying the timbered hills and vales adjacent to the Missouri River and tracking the rough country to the south in the Crooked Creek drainage. Elk also find habitat to their liking among the pines and slopes near the Musselshell River.

North of the Missouri River, from Highway 191 eastward to Timber Creek near the boundary between Phillips and Valley counties, elk are found in the breaks close to the river, but some animals also disperse into the hilly ridges to the north. Near the center of this region, adjacent to Fort Peck Lake, the UL Bend Wilderness provides elk protection from motor-vehicle disturbance. Just west of Timber Creek, the Larb Hills include steep inclines, deep ravines, and scattered stands of evergreens. Elk move back and forth between these hills and the shores of Fort Peck Lake.

Elk also occupy the north side of Fort Peck Lake from Timber Creek east to Duck Creek Bay, not far from the Fort Peck Dam. As is typical of the Missouri Breaks region, these animals are most prevalent in the hilly country adjacent to the lake.

To summarize elk distribution in this region, a couple of general observations are worthy of note. Elk densities are generally higher as one moves from east to west on both sides of Fort Peck Lake. Toward the west, elk are quite willing to swim the Missouri River, yielding some interchange between populations that many would assume are segregated by water.

Where to Hunt

Elk hunters have multiple venues for accessing this sprawling region. Public lands on the Charles M. Russell NWR are open to hunting, and other BLM and state lands further enhance the opportunities. Additionally, numerous block management properties host hunters each fall. Block management acres may top 250,000 in any given autumn, though not all of these occur in elk habitat. However, it's worth checking the block management roster to find properties that house elk.

No matter where you hunt, prudence dictates careful attention to weather, the remote nature of this region, and the unique character of the terrain, which requires special precautions for vehicle travel. Locally

The Missouri Breaks area is one of the most popular bowhunting destinations in Montana.

known as "gumbo," the soils in the Missouri Breaks area become extremely slick when wet, turning to a gooey clay that adheres to the soles of boots in great clumps and fills the wheel wells of vehicles. With the exception of graveled roads, vehicle routes become impassable when wet. Many hunters have learned through unfortunate experience the hazards of gumbo, finding themselves literally stuck at a remote campsite, waiting for the ground to dry. Tire chains are an absolute necessity, but even chained-up vehicles are no match for steep hillsides heavy with wet gumbo. Once the ground freezes, travel becomes easier, but if you get stuck in the mud or snow, the services of a tow vehicle are a long—and expensive—way away, and the cell phone on your belt may not receive reception for a call.

East of the Dry Arm of Fort Peck Lake and south of the Missouri River, either-sex elk can be taken on a general season tag in HDs 650, 651, and 652. Although some local hunters may deliberately target wapiti in this area, most animals are probably taken by deer or antelope hunters who happen to have an elk tag in their pocket or landowners who know the whereabouts of a particular herd.

From west of the Dry Arm to the Musselshell River, several routes of good access lead to public lands. All elk hunting in HD 700, which covers this area, is by special permit. Archery hunters can choose this district as an over-the-counter tag, but antlerless and either-sex tags for the general season are issued through a drawing.

From State Highway 200, about nine miles west of its intersection with State Highway 24, Van Norman Road heads north along Big Dry Creek, providing access to large blocks of BLM and state land west of the Dry Arm of Fort Peck Lake. Some five miles east of Jordan on Highway 200, Haxby Road winds for fifty miles toward the finger of land between the Dry Arm of Fort Peck and Gilbert Creek Bay. Hell Creek Road, which runs north of Highway 200 at Jordan, also accesses BLM and public land on the Charles M. Russell NWR. From Jordan, Brusett Road heads west, meandering toward the UL Bend portion of Fort Peck Lake. Several routes, such as Snow Creek Road, branch to the north from Brusett Road, providing access to the rough breaks immediately south of Fort Peck Lake. Elk are scattered and mobile across this region. Hunters are advised to work the rugged, timbered areas close to the lake, especially in the Hell Creek area and to the west.

West of the Musselshell River, elk are numerous in HD 410, which runs north from Highway 200, east of Highways 19 and 191, and south of the Missouri River/Fort Peck Lake. Like other Missouri Breaks hunting districts, HD 410 is a "draw-only" area for nearly all elk hunting. With its robust elk population and reputation for large bulls, drawing odds for either-sex general-season tags run about forty to one.

Feasible access to this area comes from several directions. From Highway 200 at Winnett, the Dovetail-Valentine Road heads north. About fifteen miles from Winnett, the roads separate, with the right-hand (east) fork, Dovetail Road, continuing north until it dead-ends at a {T} to form Dovetail Trail Road (Trail Road). The eastern branch of this road and Crooked Creek Road, found just a mile from the {T}, offer access to public lands along the Musselshell River and Crooked Creek. Just south of the Missouri River, access is also possible on the east side of Highway 191 onto the Charles M. Russell NWR.

North of the Missouri River/Fort Peck Lake, 600-series hunting districts 621, 622, 631, and 632 fall along the Missouri Breaks, with some elk also found north of these core units in districts 620 and 630. All elk hunting in these HDs requires a special permit, with odds of drawing a general tag in the more popular districts often falling below 3 percent.

On the western side, access to this area is easily gained from Bell Ridge Road (CMR Auto Nature Tour Road), just a mile north of the Fred Robinson Bridge on the Missouri River. Look for this route on the east side of Highway 191. The road parallels the river for about ten miles, then turns north to reconnect with Highway 191. A bit further north, Dry Fork Road departs Highway 191 at DY Junction about fifteen miles north of the Fred Robinson Bridge. This road passes through some private land but also gives access to some large blocks of BLM ground, with a number of spur routes leading south toward the timbered breaks adjacent to the Missouri River. Of particular note is Midale Road, which heads south from the Dry Fork Road some twenty-eight miles from Highway 191. Midale Road offers access in the vicinity of the UL Bend portion of the Charles M. Russell NWR.

Moving eastward, the UL Bend area, including the UL Bend Wilderness (which offers a backcountry environment for elk hunters), can be accessed from Sun Prairie Road. Several routes lead to Sun Prairie, but one of the most straightforward launches is from Malta, which is located at the junction of U.S. Highway 2 and Highway 191. In Malta, take South Fifth Avenue about five miles south to Content Road. About six miles south, veer right on Sun Prairie Road, then proceed a dusty forty miles or so to the boundary of the Charles M. Russell NWR. Most folks target the breaks adjacent to Fort Peck Lake, but don't overlook BLM land in the hills of the Fourchette Creek area to the west.

Although most elk in the Missouri Breaks are found fairly close to the Missouri River/Fort Peck Lake, the Larb Hills northeast of the UL Bend area provide enough security to hold wapiti as well. Two popular routes into this area include Larb Creek Road and Willow Creek South Road. Larb Creek Road runs south from Saco on Highway 2 for nearly fifty miles before arriving at the rough country around Timber Creek. If you hunt this area, please be aware that private land is interspersed with BLM and state sections.

From Timber Creek to the eastern edge of elk country north of Fort Peck Lake, Willow Creek South Road is the major point of entry. This

Table 4-1 Missouri Breaks

	Low	Moderate	High	Very High
Elk Numbers		●		
Hunters Per Square Mile*	●			
Hunters Per Elk*	●			
Trophy Potential^			●	
Remote/Roadless Areas		●		

* Hunting pressure is much higher during archery season.
^ Special tag required.

route heads west from Highway 24 a few miles west of Fort Peck. A handful of well-used spur roads heads south of South Willow Creek Road, offering access to public lands near the lake.

And speaking of the lake, remember that access to Missouri Breaks country is sometimes easier by boat on Fort Peck Reservoir than rubber tire. A rainstorm won't bother you much in a boat if you take reasonable precautions, though it might strand you in the area's gumbo goo for several days if you drive into the backcountry. However, ice floes and freeze-up must be considered by boaters as the season progresses.

Hunting Strategies

Although virtually all the elk-hunting opportunities in the Missouri Breaks region require a special elk tag, archers can obtain a permit to hunt a specific district on an over-the-counter basis. Given the Breaks' reputation for mature trophy bulls, bowhunting is extremely popular, to the point that a considerable percentage of resident hunters have complained about overcrowding.

Currently, over 50 percent of the bull elk taken from the Missouri Breaks fall to arrows. However, the success rate among bowhunters is quite low. Usually it's only those who are exceptionally skilled with their equipment and are experienced elk hunters who score on a big Breaks bull. But as is the case in all hunting, luck plays a role as well.

With heavy human activity in the area during bow season, blowing a mouth bugle to attract a bull isn't the hunter's best bet. Bugling is a useful tool if used sparingly, especially around dawn, to locate a bull. However, spot-and-stalk strategies are favored among competent archers who hunt the Breaks.

In arid years wise hunters focus on water sources. These certainly involve the Missouri River/Fort Peck Lake where elk descend to drink but also include stock tanks and other water holes. Scouting a watering area, then setting up an ambush from a ground blind or tree stand is a workable tactic.

While most bowhunters favor the peak of the breeding season, which generally occurs from mid- to late September, some seasoned archers actually prefer to hunt at a later date. Fewer cows are coming into heat in the early weeks of October, meaning bulls may be more apt to respond to a well-blown bugle or the bleat of a cow call. Also, daytime temperatures are a bit cooler, making elk more active during the day. In the Missouri Breaks region, those who hunt later in the archery season also see some-what fewer hunters afield.

Outstanding bulls like this one track the Missouri Breaks. To hunt them with a rifle, it takes a special tag. Feeling lucky?

For rifle hunters the greatest hurdle to stopping a bull is pulling the long-odds either-sex tag. Many resident hunters view the acquisition of a Breaks tag as highly as they view a similar lucky draw in the lottery. Nonetheless, some rifle hunters go home empty-handed each fall or find themselves too quick on the trigger. Beating the thirty-to-one odds in the elk-tag lottery doesn't mean you'll get a shot at a bull if you don't work at it. If you're really aiming for a trophy, be sure to educate yourself as to what exceptional antlers look like on an elk. I've heard of many folks who shot what they believed were trophy Breaks bulls, only to see the "big one" as they ferried their average animal to the pickup.

5

SOUTHEAST, EAST CUSTER NATIONAL FOREST

-------------◆-------------

Geographical Overview

Southeastern Montana is an unpredictable amalgam of low mountains, contorted badlands, and prairie. Sparse vegetation, including short grass, sagebrush, and prickly pear cactus, occurs over most of the area. Deciduous trees such as cottonwood, green ash, and chokecherry grow along the creek and river bottoms. Ponderosa pines dominate the evergreen communities, intermingled with junipers. Surface water in the form of creeks, rivers, and springs is very limited. Water for livestock (and elk) commonly comes from man-made reservoirs and stock tanks fed from wells and windmills.

Elk Distribution

Roughly 50 percent of this region provides reasonable habitat for elk. Currently, elk range across about 25 percent of it. Biologists estimate that around a thousand elk live here, with the majority found between the Tongue and Powder rivers south of U.S. Highway 212. The Custer National Forest, which nearly spans the territory between the two rivers in places, offers the easiest public access and harbors fair numbers of elk. Most of the national forest consists of ponderosa pine forest, occasionally broken by open hillsides. Old and newer burns have occurred in many places, which often provide young, tender forage for elk.

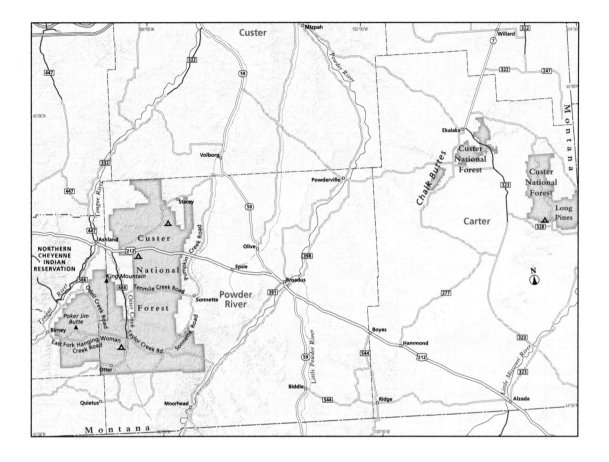

Along both the Tongue and Powder rivers, steep breaks weave up and away from the streams to the adjacent hills. Elk inhabit these areas as well as the more heavily treed pine forests. Private lands dominate these river breaks, although BLM and state lands provide some hunting access. A number of area block management properties also allow limited elk hunting.

Beyond this core area of elk habitat between the rivers, wapiti are found in fair numbers in other locations. West of the Tongue River, elk roam the eastern portion of the Wolf Mountains near the Crow Indian Reservation. A growing herd of elk also ranges in the Pine Ridge area east of Billings, south of the Yellowstone River. However, as the vast majority of their range is on private land, this is essentially a nonhuntable population for the public.

Not far from the South Dakota border, elk are repopulating two small units of the Custer National Forest: the Long Pines area and the hills and buttes near Ekalaka. Both of these areas consist of pine-covered hills interspersed with badlands and prairie. Long Pines burned extensively not too long ago, clearing large portions of habitat previously covered with timber. These burned areas are a mixture of open parks, moist draws with young stands of quaking aspen, and large expanses of youthful ponderosa pines, which provide cover for big game. Although a relatively small area, Long Pines represents very good habitat for elk. However, as is the case in most of southeastern Montana, the MDFWP manages the herd for low numbers to reduce conflicts between elk and agricultural interests. If you have an elk tag and happen to be in the area, Long Pines is worth hunting. However, planning an elk hunt that focuses solely on this area isn't recommended.

Where to Hunt

The Custer National Forest south of Ashland represents the largest contiguous area of public land open to elk hunters in this region. Road access

Stag Rock rises from the prairie breaks in the Custer National Forest south of Ashland. Fascinating rock formations make this a unique destination for elk hunters.

is good on the Custer. County and Forest Service roads crisscross the national forest at regular intervals, with two-track vehicle routes leading from these main routes. Unsigned, illegal four-wheel and OHV trails are also present in some locations. If you hunt the Custer, remember that just because there's a vehicle trail doesn't mean it's legally open for travel.

Also respect the weather and terrain. Each season, four-wheeling hotshots push too far into the backwoods only to find themselves stuck or forced to slide from the high country onto adjacent private land, an act of desperation that's illegal and creates extremely hard feelings between hunters and landowners. In general, the major roads that traverse the area are passable to a car or two-wheel-drive pickup when it's dry. When wet, even these main roads become very slippery with mud, necessitating a four-wheel-drive vehicle. It takes little moisture to render most of the primitive Forest Service roads impassable. If there's precipitation in the forecast, leave your vehicle adjacent to one of the major roads and hike— it may save you the frustration of a much longer trek from a stuck vehicle and will keep the damp landscape from becoming chewed by tire tracks.

Three major routes lead from Highway 212 east of Ashland to the Custer National Forest. The Ashland-Birney Road (566) runs south from Ashland, providing entry to the west side of the national forest near the Tongue River. Four miles east of Ashland, Otter Creek Road (484) runs south, bisecting the east and west portions of the Custer. Approximately sixteen miles east of Ashland, look for Pumpkin Creek Road south of Highway 212 for access on the east side.

To the west, Odell Creek Road veers southeast into the national forest about ten miles south of Ashland from the Ashland-Birney Road. This route eventually connects with Cow Creek/East Fork Hanging Woman Creek Road that runs east-west between Ashland-Birney Road and Otter Creek Road. Further south, look for Lee Creek Road that winds to the southeast through the southern portion of the national forest. Each of these routes provides direct hunting access to national forest lands but occasionally crosses private inholdings, which cannot be legally crossed by hunters. Primitive Forest Service roads, too numerous to mention, branch out from these main access points. In general, you'll find elk holed up in rough country, as far as they can get from human activity. Remember, though, that elk are extremely scattered in this region. If you

Table 5-1 Southeast

	Low	Moderate	High	Very High
Elk Numbers*	●			
Hunters Per Square Mile	●			
Hunters Per Elk	●			
Trophy Potential^			●	
Remote/Roadless Areas		●		

* Locally higher in good habitat.
^ Special tag required for general season. Elk may be difficult to find on public land.

don't find the elusive tan ungulates or their fresh sign in what looks like an otherwise perfect area, move on.

Otter Creek essentially bisects the Custer National Forest south of Highway 212. Private lands dominate along the northern portion of the creek, but about sixteen miles south of Highway 212, Otter Creek Road enters the national forest. To the east, look for excellent access to public land from Tenmile Creek and Fifteenmile Creek roads that wind east of Otter Creek Road to Pumpkin Creek Road. About a mile south of the Fort Howe Ranger Station, Taylor Creek Road traverses the southern part of the national forest, connecting with Sonnette Road, which eventually meets Pumpkin Creek Road further north. Many primitive roads branch from these main arteries, providing four-wheel-drive access within hiking distance of any reasonable destination in the national forest.

From the southern border of the Custer National Forest to the Wyoming border, scattered parcels of BLM and state land are open to public hunting. Although many of these encompass only a square mile, elk are sometimes found in these areas. A few years ago a friend of mine found an excellent bull while hunting a small parcel of state land. The terrain is gentler in this area than in much of the national forest, with rolling hills and shallow ravines. Look for elk in the cover provided by stands of ponderosa pines that are sprinkled throughout this area.

Hunting Strategies

Hunting elk in this region is a unique experience for a number of reasons. For one thing it's an area of sometimes startling beauty, with multicolored soils, fascinating rock formations, and picturesque vegetation woven in an unforgettable tapestry of wonder. It's also noted for large bulls that claim top mating rights in the elk herd. But perhaps most important to the hunter unfamiliar with the area is the effort required to find the elk. With so much country and relatively few animals, it takes plenty of legwork and sleuthing to locate wapiti.

With these factors in mind, hunters are advised to spend plenty of time on the go, scouting for elk or their sign. In early morning and late evening, set up on a prominent feature of the landscape from which you can see a large expanse of terrain and ply your binoculars in search of elk. During the day, hike productive areas looking for fresh tracks, droppings, or rubs that indicate elk are in the area. However, if you find fresh sign

Some big bulls roam the National Forest between the Tongue and Powder Rivers. Don't expect to find them far from cover.

during the day, it's sometimes wise to return during the evening or morning to do your hunting when animals are likely to be on their feet and more visible to humans.

In some locations, especially on the creek bottoms where hay crops are grown, elk descend onto private land to feed, then retreat to higher ground in the Custer National Forest to bed during the day. Dry years, when natural forage is less plentiful, are ideal times to look for elk adjacent to agricultural areas. Additionally, droughty seasons also reduce the number of water sources available for elk at natural springs and creeks. If it's very dry, pinpointing watering areas (including stock tanks) may also put you in elk.

6

SNOWY MOUNTAINS,
BULL MOUNTAINS,
YELLOWSTONE RIVER BREAKS

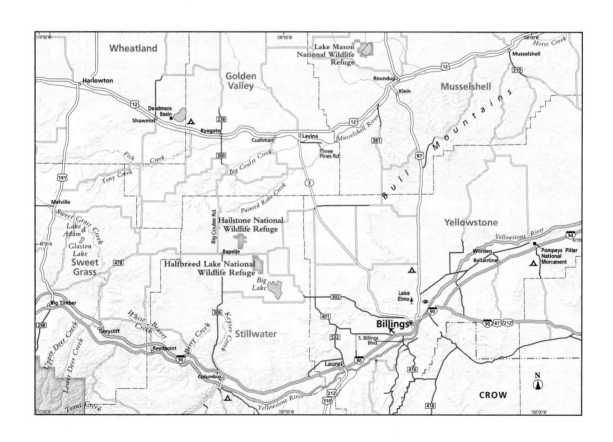

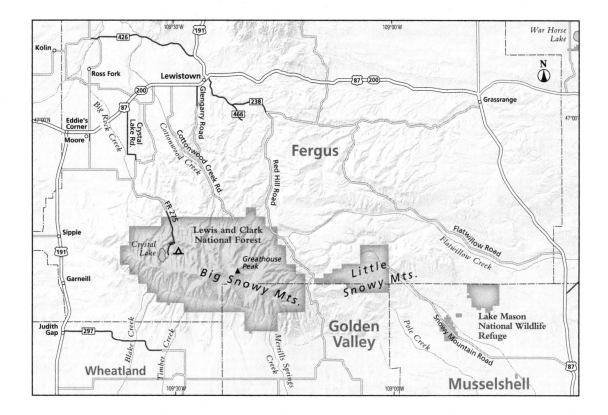

Geographical Overview

Prairie lands comprise most of central Montana, but two areas of very different topography create havens for elk.

The first is found in the Bull Mountains south of Roundup and the hilly terrain north of the Yellowstone River from Laurel to Big Timber. Although the Bull Mountains are technically a "mountain" range, most native Montanans are more apt to see them as an extended series of high hills. Maximum elevation reaches just over four thousand feet above sea level, with an elevation gain of less than a thousand feet above the surrounding prairie. Portions of the Bull Mountains are heavily forested in ponderosa pine trees, though fires dating back to the 1980s have cleared large expanses of habitat.

Similarly, the hill country north of the Yellowstone River supports heavy growth of ponderosas in many areas. However, wildfires are steadily reducing forest cover in this region as well. Stands of pines surrounded by

The Big Snowy Mountains are found in prairie country at the geographic center of Montana.

pasture or farmland typically remain intact, but due to low precipitation levels and summer heat, fires that start in major areas of forest often burn fast and hot. Even small fires normally consume hundreds of acres.

Just south of Lewistown, right smack in the geographical center of the Treasure State, the Big Snowy Mountains loom above the prairie, culminating in a lofty, east-west ridge that soars over eight thousand feet above sea level. Greathouse Peak rises to nearly eighty-seven hundred feet. From its summit on a clear day, a sharp-eyed hiker can survey the breadth of Montana. To the northwest, the Sweetgrass Hills are visible not many miles from the Canadian border. Looking south, the upthrust of the Absaroka and Pryor mountains is easily visible, just north of Wyoming.

Precious metal deposits are lacking in the Big Snowies, a factor that has buffered them from the extensive mining activity that degraded other nearby mountain ranges in the nineteenth century. Although the mountains are thickly timbered, commercial timber harvest has been minimal. These two factors yield a mountain range with a wild, unspoiled character highly treasured by local citizens and the hardy recreationists drawn to the Big Snowy backcountry.

East of the Big Snowy Mountains, the Little Snowies extend to the plains in a series of winsome foothills, dotted with evergreens, sparkling stands of quaking aspen, and lush grass. In terms of elk habitat, the Little Snowies surpass their big brother.

Elk Distribution

Bull Mountain elk range primarily on private land. MDFWP estimates that just slightly more than 10 percent of the area occupied by elk occurs on public land, mostly scattered parcels of state lands intermingled with private. Elk occasionally cross to the north side of the Musselshell River, but the vast majority of animals stay to the south. Most Bull Mountain wapiti range in a geographic area that's easy to identify. Look to the portion of Musselshell County found south of the Musselshell River, and there you'll find elk. On the west side, though, a number of elk occupy the vicinity of Painted Robe Creek, just west of the Musselshell county line. Similarly, elk habitat extends slightly east of the county line in the Horse Creek area.

Elk population in the Bull Mountains boomed in the 1990s. In 1992 biologists estimated that around two hundred animals tracked the region. Ten years later the count had shot up to nearly a thousand.

Pinpointing the scattered herds that roam the hill country north of the Yellowstone River in this region remains difficult. However, as a general rule, anywhere there's enough timber cover and a buffer from human activity, it's possible to find elk. Reports of wandering wapiti even come from coulees and timbered knobs in the area associated with the upper reaches of Canyon Creek, which holds more than a few large subdivisions of small ranchettes.

Between Columbus and Reed Point, a resident elk herd makes its home north of the Yellowstone River between Keyser Creek and White Beaver Creek, with most animals preferring the central portion of the area in the Berry Creek drainage. Further west, the territory between White Beaver Creek and Sweetgrass Creek also holds elk, with habitat extending north from the Yellowstone River for roughly fifteen miles. A more isolated but stable population of animals occurs in the Fish Creek–Tony Creek area some ten miles south of Shawmut.

In the Big Snowy Mountains, most elk graze the foothills, putting them on private land or on narrow segments of public land between private ranches and the steep, marginal habitat found in the heart of the range. Larger expanses of better habitat extend more from the north side of the mountains than the south. Even at that, the Big Snowies don't hold large numbers of elk. Though they cover much less area, the Little Snowies to the east harbor nearly twice as many wapiti.

On the north side of the "big" range, elk are scattered throughout the upper reaches of Big Rock, Cottonwood, and Big creeks. Wapiti also drift back and forth along a divide of sorts between the Big Snowies and Little Snowies formed by Red Hill Road, which runs south of Lewistown to Lavina.

The south side of the Big Snowies is noticeably drier than the north, with lighter forest cover. Nonetheless, elk are found along the numerous creeks (some flowing only seasonally) that drain the mountains. Available habitat extends from around Merrills Spring Creek on the east, westward to the East and West Forks of Blake Creek.

Though they appear to this observer as merely a lower extension of the Big Snowy Mountains, the Little Snowies are named separately on most maps. Much of this country lies between five thousand and fifty-five hundred feet above sea level and receives good rainfall, creating perfect growing conditions for grass, deciduous and coniferous trees, and shrubs—ideal habitat for elk.

For orientation purposes the Little Snowies can be roughly divided into three regions. To the north, one portion consists of north-flowing tributaries that begin in the mountains, then empty into the South Fork of McDonald Creek. (No, I don't know if the creek was named for an old-timer who farmed in the area.) Another section includes the central portion of the range, delineated by the North and South Forks of Flatwillow Creek and their tributaries, which wander eastward from the high country. The southern portion of the range lies in the slightly more arid vicinity drained by Cameron, Pole, and Willow creeks and their tributaries.

Where are the elk? In the Little Snowies that question takes minimal explanation. Nearly anywhere you find a patch of timber you'll likely find elk. East of the contiguous mountains, small herds also hole up in sheltered draws and remote areas near the headwaters of Yellow Water Creek southeast of Grass Range.

Where to Hunt

Though good numbers of elk—some say too many elk in places—range across pockets of the central Montana landscape, don't assume it's always a friendly place for public hunters. Most elk are found on private land, some of it held by landowners who primarily purchased the property for their own hunting or by traditional ranchers who lease their acreage to

From the Snowy Mountains to the Yellowstone River Breaks, ambitious bow-hunters find fine hunting for trophy bulls.

outfitters. Elk hunting is possible but takes more advance planning and mapwork than is required in many other parts of the state.

Another item of note regarding this region is the elk-management structure that tips hunting opportunities in favor of bowhunters. Every district in this region (HDs 411, 500, 511, 530, and 590) currently offer archery either-sex elk hunting on a general license but restrict either-sex hunting during the general season to those drawing a special tag. Since mature bulls polish their antlers on saplings nearly everywhere there are elk, these five hunting districts are quite popular with bowhunters.

In the Bull Mountains, public access to elk is extremely difficult. A few public roads border or bisect parcels of state land, but these typically cover one square mile or less, severely limiting the prospects of good hunting. A handful of block management properties currently lies on the edges of elk habitat, opening but a tiny percentage of the Bull Mountain elk to public harvest.

The area north of the Yellowstone River between Big Timber and Columbus poses even tougher access to public lands than the Bull Mountains. A few scattered sections of state land are found in this region, but those that are publicly accessible are very few. However, cooperation with private landowners via the block management program is fairly good, yielding some opportunity for elk hunting by hunters who don't have an individual connection to area landowners. A number of block management properties currently provide access to the elk in the Fish Creek–Tony Creek area south of Shawmut as well.

Table 6-1 Bull Mountains, Yellowstone River Breaks

	Low	Moderate	High	Very High
Elk Numbers*	●			
Hunters Per Square Mile	●			
Hunters Per Elk		●		
Trophy Potential^			●	
Remote/Roadless Areas	●			

* Locally higher in good habitat.
^ Special tag required for general season. Elk may be difficult to find on public land.

Although public land abounds in the Big Snowy Mountains and one modest segment of the Lewis and Clark National Forest is also found in the Little Snowies, elk hunting on public lands remains a rather difficult proposition. The majority of animals killed each fall comes from private lands, where access by public hunters is limited. At this writing a few ranches that hold elk on the southwest side of the Big Snowies participate in the block management program. Access to private land for elk hunting in the Little Snowies is essentially nonexistent for the average hunter, although the MDFWP would like to increase opportunities via block management or other programs.

Nonetheless, public access to portions of the Lewis and Clark National Forest found in the Snowy ranges yields reasonable opportunities for ambitious elk hunters. On the northwest side of the Big Snowy Mountains, the Crystal Lake area receives fairly heavy use from summertime visitors and also provides easy access for elk hunters. To reach this area, take U.S. Highway 191 south from U.S. Highway 87 (State Highway 200) at Eddies Corner about four miles south to Sipple. Watch for national forest access signs on the east side of the highway. Take this country road east for about ten miles until its intersection with Crystal Lake Road (FR 275). Head approximately seven miles south to the boundary of the national forest. The road continues another six miles or so to Crystal Lake Campground, but better elk hunting is typically found to the east and west shortly after the road enters the national forest.

A second access option on the north side of the Big Snowies springs from a trailhead on Cottonwood Creek. This route offers no motorized access to public lands and requires a one-and-a-half-mile hike through private land before reaching the Lewis and Clark National Forest. To reach this trailhead, take Glengarry Road south of Highway 87 about six miles west of Lewistown. Proceed about two miles, then veer east onto Cottonwood Creek Road, which continues south roughly fourteen miles to the trailhead. Look for the best hunting just inside the national forest boundary to the east and west.

On the east side of the Big Snowies, several access points to public lands are found along Red Hill Road. At Lewistown, look for State Highway 238 (Red Hill Road) south of Highway 87. A winding drive of around twenty-five miles leads to the vicinity of the national forest, where

Table 6-2 Snowy Mountains Area

	Low	Moderate	High	Very High
Elk Numbers		●		
Hunters Per Square Mile	●			
Hunters Per Elk	●			
Trophy Potential^			●	
Remote/Roadless Areas	●			

^ Special tag required for general season. Difficult hunting on public land.

the route roughly parallels the NF boundary for about ten miles. Watch for signs that indicate public access on the west side of the road to the Lewis and Clark National Forest. Hike-in hunting is possible from these points—frequenting isolated pockets of habitat will maximize your odds of downing a Big Snowy elk.

Two routes to national forest lands are also found on the south side of these mountains. East of Highway 191 at Judith Gap, State Highway 297 (Road 191N19E) heads across the prairie. About eight miles from Highway 191, watch for County Road 145 just beyond Blake Creek. This road heads north to Forest Road 8935, which leads to a trailhead near Browns Gulch, just west of Neil Creek. Another four miles down Highway 297, County Road 148 leads north to the national forest along Timber Creek. There's limited elk habitat in these areas, and elk are often found on private land rather than public.

In the Little Snowy Mountains, roughly twenty-two square miles of public land are readily accessible for elk hunting. About 95 percent of this available acreage is in the Lewis and Clark National Forest; the rest is state land. Two major access routes lead to the Little Snowies from the east, then meet in a loop that swings through the national forest. The first of these is Snowy Mountain Road, which departs from U.S. Highway 87 about sixteen miles north of Roundup. Turn west, and proceed roughly twenty-six miles to the national forest boundary. About fifteen miles north of Snowy Mountain Road on Highway 87, Flatwillow Road runs west along Flatwillow Creek. Roughly twenty-three miles from the highway, watch for Forest Road 271 on the south side of the road.

Although twenty-two square miles represents a fair-size chunk of land, this piece of the national forest real estate in the Little Snowies suffers from too much vehicle access. Vehicle travel is restricted to designated routes, but you'll search hard for an acre of land that's much more than a mile from an open road—certainly not the best situation for elk hunting.

Hunting Strategies

In general, this region probably isn't the best option for nonresident hunters, unless they're employing the services of an outfitter or have connections for hunting private land. However, given the restrictive bull harvest during the general season, potential for killing an older-age bull is quite good—if you find elk. Because of the area's limited potential for hunting public land, be sure to check what's available in the block management program to augment opportunities on traditional public lands.

Bowhunters enjoy essentially unlimited opportunity for hunting on a general tag in this region and possess other advantages as well. When hunting small parcels of public land, the bugles and rubs of a rutting bull are very helpful in locating an available animal. In the Big Snowy Mountains, elk are more likely found on public land during the archery season than the general season.

Locals or other resident hunters who frequent this region are advised to keep tabs on small parcels of state land in the Bull Mountains. Big bulls are occasionally killed in these spots, which are sometimes overlooked by many hunters. I once spotted a tremendous six-point bull on an isolated but publicly accessible section of state land the opening day of general season, though unfortunately, I wasn't carrying the special tag required to take a bull.

7

ABSAROKA MOUNTAINS

-----------◆-----------

Geographical Overview

Dominated by the highlands of the Absaroka-Beartooth Wilderness area in the Absaroka Range, this region represents some of the most beautiful, rugged, and remote country in the state of Montana (and the nation).

Of the nearly one million acres in the Absaroka-Beartooth Wilderness, a considerable percentage is found above timberline at elevations exceeding ten thousand feet. Over much of this mountain range, steep slopes rise to expansive plateaus and jagged peaks. Water abounds, in the form of numerous alpine lakes and countless creeks. To each point of the compass, the Absaroka Range melds to the lowlands in an amalgam of ridges and foothills that descend from the mountains. The open hillsides and sheltered bowls of the foothills provide essential winter range for elk, deer, moose, and bighorn sheep. In 1988 the infamous wildfires that seared Yellowstone National Park also burned extensively in the Absaroka-Beartooth Wilderness. Several major fires have ignited since, but the long-term results of these blazes are positive for large ungulates like elk.

Given the elevation and remote character of the Absaroka Range, fall weather can be severe and unpredictable. Precipitation that shows up as rain in the valleys may dump ten inches of snow on the peaks and passes. While hunting this range is an exceptional experience of scenic quality, there's little room for error when it comes to the weather.

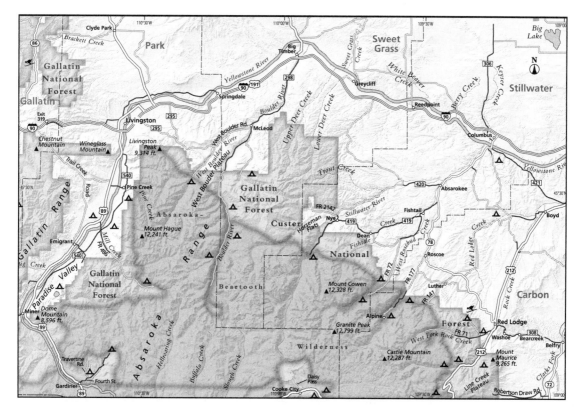

Elk Distribution

On the extreme southeastern portion of this area, several creeks drain the high country of Line Creek Plateau and Mount Maurice, carrying their water eastward to the Clark's Fork of the Yellowstone River. The terrain between the river and the face of the Absaroka Range is primarily flat and arid, which makes it a good wintering area for elk. A sizeable elk herd ranges along the slope of the mountains from the headwaters of Line Creek along the Wyoming border, north to the headwaters of Grove Creek on the east side of Mount Maurice.

West of the town of Red Lodge, elk populate the West Fork of Rock Creek and its tributaries on the slopes of Silver Run Plateau, Bare Mountain, and adjacent areas. Along the flank of the mountains from Red Lodge to West Rosebud Creek, elk range from the steep slopes down to the foothills and creek bottoms, which are often found on private land. Although elk might be found anywhere in this area, they're most com-

Snow blankets Livingston Peak in the Absaroka Range in November. Look for elk in the foothills when the weather is nasty on top.

monly associated with the upper portions of Red Lodge, Butcher, and Morris creeks. From West Rosebud Creek to the Stillwater River, similar habitat also supports an elk herd that roams along the mountains and foothills at the upper ends of Fishtail and Fiddler creeks.

Although the main stem of the Stillwater River appears to be suitable elk habitat within the Absaroka-Beartooth Wilderness, elk are notably absent from this drainage, possibly due to heavy foot and horse travel that occurs during the summer. However, a small elk herd populates the Horseman Flats vicinity, a mixed bench of open and timbered habitat between the Stillwater River and the West Fork of the Stillwater west of the microcommunity of Nye.

Elk have also been historically associated with the headwaters of Trout Creek, some eight miles north of Horseman Flats. At this writing, however, an extremely large forest fire recently burned hundreds of thousands of acres in this region. It remains to be seen how the fire's aftermath will affect the seasonal movements of elk. Wapiti in the upper reaches of the Deer Creek drainages south of Big Timber have similarly seen their home seared to the ground. Although the Derby Mountain fire had disastrous short-term consequences, elk will likely repopulate the region, possibly in increased numbers.

Perhaps the largest herd of elk found in the northern portion of the Absaroka Range occurs in the Boulder River drainage. About fifteen miles south of the tiny town of McLeod, the Boulder River leaves the mountains to wind into a winsome valley dominated by irrigated hayfields and a growing number of subdivisions. Above the vale the headwaters of the Boulder River tumble from the peaks more than thirty miles away. From the headwaters to the valley, a dozen or more creeks swell the waters of the river from both sides, typically flowing from narrow valleys above the river.

Throughout the summer and fall, elk populate these vales, grazing among small aspen groves and lush meadows, and bedding in the evergreens for shade and shelter. As snow builds in the high valleys during mid- to late fall, elk move down along the Boulder River onto their winter range.

On the opposite side of the West Boulder Plateau, a nearly identical situation exists on the West Boulder River. A sizeable elk herd utilizes the West Boulder drainage and its tributaries, wintering primarily on private land around Ellis Basin. Elk are also found in the Mount Greeley area at the headwaters of Greeley Creek. Not far to the west, wapiti inhabit the creek bottoms and timbered slopes of Livingston Peak and Shell Mountain.

The river bottom that separates the Absaroka and Gallatin ranges is known as Paradise Valley. Watch the setting sun cast its watercolors of light on and above the peaks of the Absaroka Range, and it's easy to surmise why the valley was so named. The Yellowstone River winds through Paradise Valley, with several tributaries from the west face of the Absarokas feeding the great stream.

One of these feeder streams, Mill Creek, runs some twenty miles from its headwaters before leaving the mountains on the east side of Paradise Valley. A considerable herd of elk occupies the Mill Creek drainage and its many tributaries. As is typical of elk in mountain habitats, these animals hang high in the upper basins and valleys during the summer, drifting down in the fall toward Paradise Valley, where they winter on the open slopes and sheltered breaks above the Yellowstone River. Elk are also spread along the lower slopes and foothills of the Absaroka Range north and south of Mill Creek, northward to the Pine Creek area, southward to the vicinity of Dome Mountain and Cedar Creek.

A final elk population inhabits Montana's portion of the Absaroka Range north of Yellowstone National Park. Near Gardiner, the upstream portion of the Yellowstone River flows roughly east-west before bending southward near the confluence of the Lamar River north of Tower Junction. North of the Yellowstone and Lamar rivers, several important tributaries including Hellroaring, Buffalo, and Slough creeks drain the uplands of this portion of the Absaroka Range. Migratory elk herds populate these drainages in the summer, moving to winter range along the lowlands near the Yellowstone River in late fall. Although viable numbers of elk still roam this area, the size of the herd has dropped dramatically since the reintroduction of wolves to Yellowstone National Park in the mid-1990s.

Where to Hunt

On the extreme southeastern side of the Absaroka Range, the best public access is from Robertson Draw Road (FR 2008). This road is found just north of the Wyoming border on State Highway 72. From the highway, turn west on Robertson Draw Road and proceed about ten miles to the boundary of the Custer National Forest. Hunt west and north, paying close attention to your location. To the north it's easy to stray onto private land; to the south and west, be careful not to cross the state line into Wyoming. In addition to this public access, cooperation with local ranchers in the block management program has an excellent history in this area. Opportunities for antlerless elk hunting in this HD 520 area are good for those who draw the required tag. Hunting for bulls also requires a draw-only tag and offers a fine hunt for those who find luck in the lottery. Currently, this area has very reasonable odds for a draw-only bull hunt compared to other parts of the state, with around 20 percent of resident applicants securing the tag.

Between Red Lodge and West Rosebud Creek, several access points are available for public hunting in HD 520. West of Red Lodge, take FR

71 up the West Fork of Rock Creek to hunt elk in the Silver Run vicinity. Several Forest Service trails provide hike-in access from the road.

Along the eastern face of the Absarokas, access to national forest lands is somewhat limited, but a handful of roads and trailheads are found west of State Highway 78 between the communities of Red Lodge and Roscoe. Near Luther, West Red Lodge Creek Road (FR 141) allows access to national forest lands on the upper reaches of West Red Lodge Creek. From the boundary it's possible to hunt west, but don't overlook the state land to the east. Southwest of Roscoe, walk-in access can be gained from East Rosebud Creek Road (FR 177) along the flank of the mountains toward West Red Lodge Creek.

A considerable amount of national forest land lies on the lower slopes of the mountains in good elk habitat between West Rosebud Creek and the Stillwater River. However, access is somewhat difficult and involves extra effort. One option is hiking north from West Rosebud Creek Road (FR 72), which originates southwest of Fishtail on State Highway 419. Take this road to the national forest, then hunt to the northwest. Easier access is gained from Benbow Road (FR 1414), which originates just past Dean on Highway 419. A drive of about three miles puts you on national forest land. Hunt south, toward East and West Fishtail creeks.

North of the West Fork of the Stillwater River, public access to elk that roam the headwaters of Trout Creek and the Meyers Creek vicinity is available by following Limestone Road (FR 2142) northwest of Nye to the Myers Creek Ranger station. Trails fan out from this area, yielding good opportunities for foot and horseback hunting to the north and west. Before tackling this area, you might save yourself some legwork by checking with the MDFWP Region 5 headquarters to assess the status of area elk after the 2006 Derby Mountain fire. Elk habitat on the upper portions of the two branches of Deer Creek south of Big Timber can be reached via Lower Deer Creek Road (FR 482), which originates from the frontage road south of I-90 between Greycliff (exit 377) and Big Timber. But as the Derby Mountain fire also burned this area, making contact with local management sources (Region 5 MDFWP or Big Timber National Forest headquarters) is advisable before hunting.

More numerous, straightforward access options are open to those who hunt the elk herd on the main stem of the Boulder River. To reach this area, take State Highway 298 south of Big Timber. The highway follows the course of the river to the national forest, then proceeds as a gravel road some thirty miles up the drainage—the upper portions are impassable except to experienced drivers with high-clearance, four-wheel-drive vehicles. Along this road, some eight trailheads provide excellent horseback and foot access to the major creek bottoms. Look for elk in the upper basins associated with these creeks and in the flatter areas along the ridges that slope downward from the drainage divides. Bowhunting is fairly popular here, as the bugling of bulls during the mating season makes them easier to find in this remote, timbered habitat. Grizzly bears also roam this area, especially at the upper end of the drainage, so bowhunters are advised to carry pepper spray and be ever alert to their surroundings.

Across the divide, access to the West Boulder River is a little more limited. The main point of entry is found at the end of West Boulder Road. To reach this route, follow Highway 298 south of Big Timber. Turn west onto West Boulder Road just south of McLeod. Trails that branch out from the end of the road provide easy hiking to the west, north, and south. Another option for hunting slopes to the west is found at the two trailheads that begin at the forest boundary on Mission Creek and Little Mission Creek. To reach these, take Mission Creek Road (FR 295) south of I-90 about ten miles east of Livingston (exit 343).

The east side of the Absarokas in Paradise Valley holds several populations of elk, but good public access is limited. On the northern end, elk in the Livingston Peak vicinity can be hunted from Suce Creek Road (FR 201), which terminates at a trailhead at the national forest boundary. Drive U.S. Highway 89 south of Livingston for about three miles, then turn east onto State Highway 540. Follow this route about two miles, then turn east again onto Suce Creek Road.

To the south, two additional trailheads allow public access to the west slopes of the Absaroka Range at Pine Creek. These are located west of Highway 540 on Pine Creek Road (FR 202) about five miles south of Suce Creek Road. Look for elk in limited numbers north and south of the trailheads on the lower slopes.

Mill Creek, some fifteen miles south of Pine Creek, affords numerous options for elk hunting. To enter this drainage, take Mill Creek Road (FR 486) from Highway 89 about fifteen miles south of Livingston. Proceed south to where the road enters the national forest. Cross-country, hike-in hunting is available on the east side of the road, but take care to avoid trespassing on the narrow strip of private land along the creek to the west. From the national forest boundary, the road runs about ten miles up the drainage, with several trailheads offering access to tributaries of Mill Creek and elk country on the upper slopes and bowls. Fairly early in the general season, hunting pressure moves elk down the drainage onto private lands adjacent to the national forest. Southwest of Mill Creek, public access arises from Emigrant Creek Road and Sixmile Creek Road. Resident elk are sometimes found in this vicinity, but late-season hunting opportunities are best if heavy snowfall in the mountains moves elk onto the area's open slopes.

If you're up for a wilderness adventure of grand proportions, hunting the Absaroka-Beartooth Wilderness north of Yellowstone Park in HD 316 is an experience you'll remember for a lifetime. Quite honestly, hunter success rates are low, but this area has great appeal to elk hunters for several reasons. First of all, it's one of just two areas in the state that offer an early general season (rifle) that coincides with the elk rut. Second, older-age trophy bulls move between the wilderness and the national park, giving the hunter at least some chance of killing an exceptional bull if he finds elk. Finally, the opportunity to hunt unspoiled, soul-lifting scenery where grizzly bears, mountain goats, wolves, and bighorn sheep roam the ridges along with elk is rare indeed.

As the heart of HD 316 lies miles from any point of motorized access, most folks who hunt this area pack in with horses and mules, utilizing their own stock or hiring the services of an outfitter. However, hunters in top physical condition can make this a backpack hunt as well. I've tried it both ways and enjoyed myself immensely whether on foot or horseback.

From the north the most logical route begins at the Box Canyon trailhead and ranger station on the main Boulder River (see previous directions). Trail 27 follows the East Fork of the Boulder River to its source, then drops into the headwaters of Slough Creek, providing excellent access to this major drainage. From the Box Canyon trailhead, a very rough road, suitable only to experienced drivers in four-wheel-drive, high-clearance vehicles; horses; and hikers, winds up the Boulder River for about another five-and-a-half miles. This road connects with trail 32, which ascends to the top of Boulder Pass, then drops into the headwaters of Buffalo Creek.

Table 7-1 Absaroka Mountains

	Low	Moderate	High	Very High
Elk Numbers*		•		
Hunters Per Square Mile		•		
Hunters Per Elk		•		
Trophy Potential^	•			
Remote/Roadless Areas				•

* Locally higher in good habitat.
^ Higher during early rifle season north of Yellowstone Park, though hunter success rates are low.

A third access option involves trekking up trail 15 (Copper Creek) or trail 127 (Sheep Creek), then crossing the divide to the Middle Fork of Hellroaring Creek. Both of these trailheads are found west of the road above the Box Canyon trailhead. Copper Creek is roughly four miles from Box Canyon, Sheep Creek around five miles.

On the east side of HD 316, three trails lead into the wilderness from the Daisy Pass–Lake Abundance Road north of Cooke City. Trail 24 heads north along the headwaters of the Stillwater River, but better hunting is generally found to the west from trails 113 and 84, which lead to Wolverine Creek and Lake Abundance Creek, tributaries on the east side of Slough Creek.

Hunting Strategies

Outside the Absaroka-Beartooth Wilderness, elk often wind up on private land in the foothills during the general elk season, insulating them from public hunting. With this factor in mind, hunting the first few days of the season with a clear destination and strategy in mind often yields the greatest chance for success. However, elk sometimes drift back and forth between private land and national forest, so it's occasionally possible to catch them on the public side of the fence, especially if you're able to hunt midweek, when hunting pressure is low.

In the Boulder and West Boulder drainages, weather greatly affects wapiti whereabouts. A good strategy for archery or general-season hunting is to work your way up the trails and drainages until you find elk or fresh sign. Once located, hunt look-alike areas at similar elevations.

Patently unpredictable, early-winter weather that pushes elk from Yellowstone National Park to wintering areas north of Gardiner triggers exceptionally good hunting and exceptionally high pressure. If this happens, droves of orange-clad rifle toters wait near the closed buffer zone near the park, hoping a herd of bachelor bulls will come through. It's an ugly sort of hunting.

However, herds of animals also drift through the "hot" area at night. Muster the will to hike away from the firing line, and you might find a trophy bull and a much more satisfying experience to boot.

Tackling the early general season in the Absaroka-Beartooth Wilderness takes livestock and/or a strong back and legs. If you take the challenge, spend lots of time behind the binoculars at daylight and dusk,

The author scans an old burn north of Yellowstone Park. These may be ugly to view, but provide great forage for elk.

scouring the terrain. Pay special attention to the edges between burned areas and timber, as elk often find good feed on the burns, but retreat to the timber for bedding.

No matter where or how you hunt the wilderness, don't forget that bears, black and grizzly, share the mountains. You must take food storage and other precautionary measures when you camp. Additionally, if you kill an elk and can't retrieve it to camp or a trailhead right away, do what you can to reduce the chances of a bear dining on your meat. If you quarter, bone, or cape the animal for packing, accomplish those tasks immediately. Stash the meat, cape, and antlers in a visible location well away from the gut pile and carcass. When you return, watch the area carefully before you approach to make sure a bear hasn't usurped your kill. If it has, report the situation to MDFWP personnel as quickly as possible.

8

BRIDGER, CRAZY,
CASTLE MOUNTAINS

-------------◆-------------

Geographical Overview

Depending on one's route from the east, any of these three mountain ranges—Bridger, Crazy, or Castle—might be the first encountered on a westward pilgrimage across Montana. Located just northeast of Bozeman, the Bridgers are a fairly rugged expanse of mountains dominated by a lofty ridge that runs generally in a north-south direction. The mountains jut abruptly from the Gallatin Valley on the west, where wickedly steep slopes arise to high points along the backbone of the range. Sacajawea Peak, the high point in the range, thrusts 9,665 feet into the wild blue sky. The Bridgers often receive heavy snowfall in the winter, especially on the east side of the range, home to the Bridger Bowl Ski Area.

The eastern shoulders of the Bridgers catch the most snowfall, but they also flow more gently from the peaks to the plains than the west side, descending in a series of knobs, benches, and foothills that create ideal habitat for elk. The Bangtail Mountains, considered a separate range by some, lie just west of the main stem of the Bridgers on the southern end. Like the main Bridgers, the Bangtails comprise excellent elk habitat.

Slightly north but mostly east of the Bridgers, the Crazy Mountains also lie on a north-south axis. Various stories recount the naming of this range, and most of them involve a deranged woman who lived in the area. The original moniker, the "Crazy Woman Mountains," lost its female reference, yielding the current name.

At the heart of the range, the Crazies are exceedingly severe. Vertiginous slopes rise abruptly from narrow canyons to wind-scoured peaks. Mountain goats are the most plentiful ungulates of the high country,

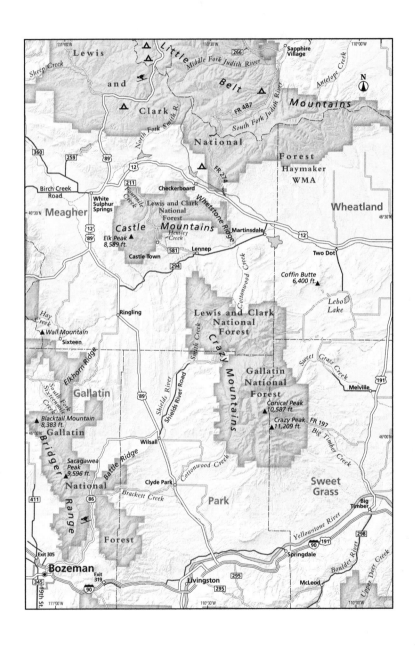

Snow falls deep on the east side of the Bridger Mountains where there are lots of elk, but access is difficult.

giving hint of the characteristic terrain. At 11,214 feet, Crazy Peak gives the range claim to the third highest group of mountains in the state.

Despite the imposing nature of the high country, the Crazy Mountains also span numerous creek bottoms and lower-lying areas that slowly meld into the prairie. Although most hunters and naturalists assume that the greatest concentrations of elk are found in the southwest, the Crazy Mountain Elk Management Unit (as identified by the MDFWP) currently boasts more elk per square mile of habitat than any other region in the state.

Just north and slightly west of the Crazies, the Castle Mountains are a small but scenic range nestled in traditional ranch country east of White Sulphur Springs. Though the mountains are somewhat steeper to the west, the Castles are generally quite easy to traverse on foot or horseback. The highest and most remote country is found around Elk Peak (8,566 feet), where a good system of nonmotorized trails provides hunting with a backcountry feel for folks willing to get out and hike. To the east, an extension of the Castles juts from the major portion of the range in a series of lower-lying ridges that terminate in the rough country around Whetstone Ridge, west of Martinsdale.

Elk Distribution

Elk roam the western flank of the Bridger Range from just north of Bozeman to the Blacktail Mountain vicinity, which is the westernmost point of the range. This portion of the Bridgers consists of steep slopes and ravines that drop sharply to agricultural lands (and now subdivisions). Elk are commonly found near this transition zone, feeding on hay, grain crops, and pasturelands in the shadows of the peaks, then retreating to the timbered slopes to bed for the day. Though plentiful, these elk spend much of their time on private land. When and where they're in the Gallatin National Forest, difficult public access makes them essentially unavailable to hunters who lack an in with a local landowner.

Similarly, good numbers of elk inhabit the northern portion of the Bridgers, in the vicinity of the South and Middle forks of Sixteenmile Creek. Like those on the west side of the range, these elk often move between feeding areas on agricultural land and higher, more timbered areas for security.

On the northeastern portion of the range, a sizeable herd of elk covers the upper slopes and foothills in the Flathead Creek drainage. This area forms something of a horseshoe shape, bounded by Elkhorn Ridge on the north and Battle Ridge on the south, two spurs that extend eastward from the main part of the Bridger Range. Elk scatter throughout this area in suitable habitat, wintering on the lowlands but drifting to higher elevations in the summer.

South of Battle Ridge, wapiti are numerous in the Brackett and Bangtail Creek drainages. Look for more elk south of these prime areas, scattered all the way to the southern end of the range near I-90 east of Bozeman. However numerous these robust elk herds are, though, public access to them is lacking. The MDFWP estimates that less than 10 percent of the elk in this area are found on public land.

Very high elk populations occur in the Crazy Mountains, where animals have greatly expanded their numbers and range in the past two decades. On the west side of the range, the elk count more than tripled in the ten-year period from 1992 to 2002. Although populations have stabilized somewhat in recent years, the Crazies offer all that's necessary for a booming elk herd-security from humans, sheltered calving areas, nutritious summer forage, and protected winter range.

On the southern end of the range, elk are found on the upper reaches of most drainages from Cottonwood Creek around the southern face of the mountains to the headwaters of Swamp Creek and the South Fork of Big Timber Creek. A very sizeable herd of elk winters in the Falls Creek–Rock Creek foothills, retreating to higher elevations in the summer and fall.

Moving northward on the east side of the mountains, wapiti wander freely among lower slopes of the range from Big Timber Creek to Sweet Grass Creek, where open meadows, moist creek bottoms, and timbered north-facing slopes create perfect habitat.

The region between Sweet Grass Creek and the tributaries of Cottonwood Creek on the northeast side of the range (West and Middle forks of Cottonwood Creek, Loco Creek) also represents superb and highly occupied elk habitat. In recent winter surveys nearly one-half the elk observed on the east side of the Crazy Mountains were found in this area. Animals are also abundant in the upper reaches of the American Fork and Big Elk Creek.

On the west side of the mountains, wapiti roam the flanks from Cottonwood Creek (almost directly south of the identically named "Cottonwood Creek" on the north side of the range) north to the headwaters of the Shields River. North of the Shields River, elk are abundant on the lower slopes of the northwest portion of the range, some inhabiting public land on the Lewis and Clark National Forest but many spending the majority of their time on private land.

In the Castle Mountains, elk concentrate in larger herds in the foothills during the winter but often scatter into smaller bands at higher elevations during the summer. Elk are found on the eastern spur of the mountains on higher portions of major creek drainages. On the south side of the range, wapiti are distributed in the upper Bonanza Creek area, east to Thomas Creek and Whetstone Ridge. Elk are also found on the southernmost flanks of the mountains in the Warm Springs Creek drainage. The Fords Creek area on the west side also supports a herd of wintering elk.

On the north side of the Castles, elk favor secluded areas on upper reaches of the Fourmile Creek drainage and are scattered eastward to the Hall Creek region. Occasionally, animals are seen west of Fourmile Creek, on slopes around the northwest side of the range, most often in the Lone Willow Creek drainage. Wapiti also wander between the southern end of

Table 8-1 Bridger Mountains

	Low	Moderate	High	Very High
Elk Numbers				●
Hunters Per Square Mile		●		
Hunters Per Elk	●			
Trophy Potential	●			
Remote/Roadless Areas		●		

the Castles and the Crazy Mountains. Similarly, animals occasionally move back and forth from the Little Belts to the Castle Mountains on the north side of the range.

Where to Hunt

Bridger Mountains

In the Bridger Mountains, the hunter's greatest challenge is not finding elk but finding access. Public lands administered by the Gallatin National Forest in the major portion of the Bridger Range are confined to a relatively narrow strip only three to six miles wide. Much of the terrain within this strip represents poor elk habitat, being too steep or above timberline. A worse situation confronts the hunter on the eastern abutment—there's some national forest land in the Battle Ridge and Bangtail mountains regions, but it's comingled with private, yielding little opportunity for hunting. Flexible local hunters find some success in the Bridgers, but if you're coming to Big Sky Country from out of state, my advice is to pitch your camp elsewhere.

That said, there are a few places an enterprising hunter might try. On the north end of the range, Flathead Creek Road (FR 6931) winds eastward over the range from the Gallatin Valley. Hunt north or south from the road—on either side, several square miles of national forest land lies in elk habitat. If you opt for this area, some preseason scouting is a worthwhile investment. To reach Flathead Creek Road from the Gallatin Valley, take Dry Creek Road north from Belgrade. A drive of roughly twenty miles leads to Flathead Creek Road. Turn right (east) and proceed about seven miles to the national forest boundary.

On the east side of the Bridgers, public access is available in the Fairy Lake area, a popular picnicking spot with the Bozeman crowd. From Bozeman, take State Highway 86 north about twenty miles to Fairy Lake Road (FR 74). About three miles west of the highway Fairy Lake Road enters the Gallatin National Forest. To the north and south, a fairly narrow strip of public land runs from private holdings to the steep face of the mountains. Ambitious hunters willing to put some miles between themselves and the roads occasionally find elk. Trail 540 yields easy hiking to the north, but your best chance of tagging an elk means getting away from human disturbance along the trail.

Crazy Mountains

Better public access for hunting is found in the Crazy Mountains, except on the eastern side, where public opportunity for elk harvest is limited by

A hunter glasses the east side of the Crazy Mountains, which boasts some of the highest elk numbers in the state.

a checkerboard pattern of national forest and private land, which severely reduces access points. However, if you're willing to spend some time in the leather of a saddle or hiking boots, it's still possible to make a hunt.

The major point of entry to national forest lands on the east side of the Crazies is found in the Big Timber Creek drainage. From U.S. Highway 191 about thirteen miles north of Big Timber, take Big Timber Creek Road (FR 25) west for about sixteen miles to Half Moon Campground. From here, it's possible to hunt south onto several sections of national forest lands, but keep a map handy, as private and public lands are interwoven in alternating blocks. Also, remember that south of Sweet Grass Creek, to the West Fork of Duck Creek on the south end of the range, which includes the Big Timber Creek drainage, hunters must secure a special tag to down a bull in district HD 580. Each season, trophy bulls are taken from this area by those lucky enough to draw the tag. General elk tags are valid only for antlerless animals—this portion of the Crazy Mountains is a good place to take meat. Outfitters and private landowners here generally don't allow public access for bulls, but some will open their properties for antlerless hunting.

Somewhat better public access exists on the north end of the mountains, where two roads offer entry into larger segments of national forest lands. West of Martinsdale on State Highway 294, Cottonwood Creek/Forest Lake Road provides easy entry to the national forest on the northeast side of the mountains. From Martinsdale, travel west on Highway 294 for about five miles. Turn left (south) on Cottonwood Creek/Forest Lake Road (FR 66). Continue roughly nine miles to the national forest boundary. Hunting via several trails that branch out from the road between the national forest boundary and the Forest Lake Campground is one available option. From the campground itself, there's good elk country to the east. Additionally, a cross-country hike from the spur road on the West Fork of Cottonwood Creek leads to fine habitat that's not particularly steep to the northwest.

On the west side, easily accessible public entry to the national forest awaits in the headwaters of the Shields River, via Shields River Road. Drive north on Shields River Road (FR 844) from U.S. Highway 89 at Wilsall for a little over twenty miles to reach the Shields River Campground area. Hunt north of the campground toward the headwaters of

Table 8-2 Crazy Mountains

	Low	Moderate	High	Very High
Elk Numbers				•
Hunters Per Square Mile		•		
Hunters Per Elk	•			
Trophy Potential^	•			
Remote/Roadless Areas		•		

^ High in southern portion of east side (HD 580). Special tag required during general season. Public access is difficult.

Dugout and Crandall Creek, or scour the numerous creek bottoms south of FR 844.

Alternatively, take FR 991, north of FR 844. FR 991 leads to the national forest in the Smith Creek area, where a half-dozen small tributaries spring from ravines well worth an elk hunter's investigation. Much of the Smith Creek drainage has vehicle travel restrictions during the general elk season, making it attractive to backcountry hunters. Elk from this area winter to the west on the foothills. Once they're pushed from the high country, you won't likely again find them on public land. This suggests better hunting during the archery season and the early part of the rifle hunt.

Some five miles southwest of the upper Shields River area as the crow flies (or the wapiti walks), another public point of entry to the Crazy Mountains is found on Porcupine Creek. From Shields River Road about ten miles north of Wilsall, Porcupine Road (FR 203) forks to the right (east). Approximately eight miles of driving leads to a Forest Service trailhead. Trail 258 runs east for about a mile, then swings north and crosses several creeks that drain into the Shields River, offering fairly easy traveling in elk habitat.

Castle Mountains

Public access to the Castle Mountains is limited to just a handful of roads but once gained is easier to navigate than much of the Crazy and Bridger

Table 8-3 Castle Mountains

	Low	Moderate	High	Very High
Elk Numbers		●		
Hunters Per Square Mile		●		
Hunters Per Elk	●			
Trophy Potential	●			
Remote/Roadless Areas		●		

ranges, as private land interspersed with public isn't as prevalent. The main point of entry is FR 221/581, which runs south to north over the mountains (FR 211 on the north side, FR 581 on the south). This route also represents the boundary between HD 452 to the west and HD 449 to the east. From the north, pick up FR 211 from U.S. Highway 12 about seven miles east of White Sulphur Springs at Fourmile Creek. From the south, FR 581 runs north of Highway 294 at Lennep, following Albaugh Creek into the mountains.

Although this road is the only public vehicle access to HD 452 to the west, a good trail system promotes backcountry travel. From FR 8886, a back road that runs west from the old mining area near the top of the mountains, trail 718 winds along the northeast-southwest-lying ridge along the crest of the range. From FR 211, several trailheads provide access to national forest lands via foot travel or horseback. Elk may be encountered nearly anywhere in this western portion of the Castles early in the fall, giving considerable advantage to bowhunters who can pinpoint the location of herds from the bugling of bulls.

Access to HD 449 east of FR 211/581 is good from FR 581, which forks from FR 211/581 near the summit of the range. Numerous vehicle trails sprout from FR 581, yielding motorized entry to much of the eastern portion of the Castles. Additionally, Bonanza Creek Road (FR 585) enters the national forest from Highway 294 directly north of Lennep. A final option involves Pasture Gulch Road (FR 694), located south of Highway 12 about six miles east of Checkerboard. This road wanders along Pasture Gulch, yielding good hunting options in the Whetstone

Ridge area. Elk might be encountered nearly anywhere in the eastern part of the Castles, but early hunting pressure frequently nudges them from the national forest onto private lands.

Hunting Strategies

Map skills and ambition are a hunter's best weapons in conquering the challenges of hunting areas with limited public access. Entry points are limited in all of these mountain ranges, so hunting pressure tends to concentrate near the ends of access roads and trailheads. Striking out a couple of miles beyond these vicinities will put you in less human company and more elk. Additionally, look for natural topographical barriers such as creeks and steep ridges (or drainage divides) that most other hunters aren't willing to cross. Hoof it into these locations, and you're more likely to find elk.

Also, acquire good maps that clearly show land ownership and learn how to read them. Oftentimes, targeting public acres near a public-private land boundary is an excellent strategy when animals are on the move or drifting back and forth between the two properties. However, it's the hunter's responsibility to stay on public land. Many hunters avoid these areas as their fear of straying onto private land makes them leery. But with current maps and good orienteering skills, there's no excuse to trespass on private lands—and no reason to avoid the edges.

Orienteering skills can be acquired through formal instruction or self-study. Educational outreach programs from colleges and local school districts sometimes offer orienteering classes. Courses are also taught by various conservation organizations or groups that promote backcountry skills. Most of these training experiences now include instruction with GPS units, which are very valuable aids in determining property boundaries. In the absence of formal training, spending a few days in the field with someone competent in orienteering should give you the basic skills, which you can then practice on your own.

9

LITTLE BELT,
HIGHWOOD MOUNTAINS

------------- ◆ -------------

Geographical Overview

Generally speaking, Montana mountains can be classified into one of two categories: the clustered, contiguous mountains of the western portion of the state and the central "island" ranges that are largely isolated from other mountains. Of the latter category, the Little Belt Mountains south of Great Falls are the largest. In fact, the Little Belts are a major range no matter how they are classified. Roughly seventy miles from east to west and sixty miles from north to south, the Little Belts cover considerably more area than the Big Belts. They also outsize the Gallatin, Madison, and Gravelly ranges to the southwest.

Despite their breadth, the Little Belts aren't a particularly high or rugged range, though some deep canyons and steep ridges lurk here and there among friendlier terrain. Big Baldy Mountain, the range's highest peak rises nearly ninety-two hundred feet above sea level, though few other mountaintops measure within a thousand feet of this barren patriarch. With ample rainfall and elevation suited to native conifers, the Little Belts are mostly forested in lodgepole pine, fir, and spruce trees.

Of the industries that are core to Montana's historic economy, all have played upon the Little Belt stage. Mining, including prospecting for famous Yogo sapphires, bears some responsibility for the area's development and prosperity. Logging also fuels the economy, though currently on a smaller scale than in previous decades. Many of the roads winding through the Lewis and Clark National Forest

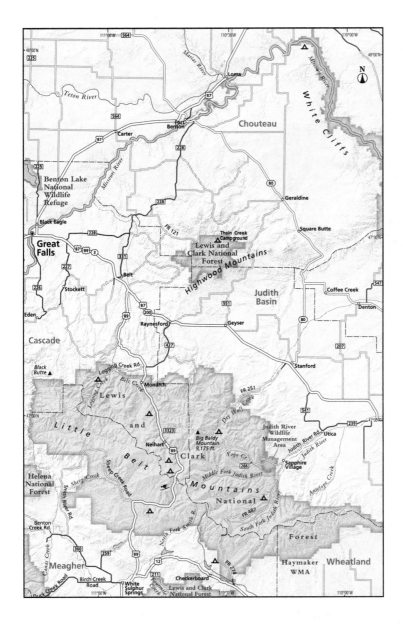

that covers most of the range were established for logging. In the foot-hills, ranching operations graze sheep and cattle—and provide winter range for numerous elk.

Northeast of the Little Belts, the Highwood Mountains appear as a mere dot on the state map but nonetheless boast excellent elk hunting in a unique geographical area. On their trek westward up the Missouri River,

Vehicle access to the Little Belt Mountains is easy, but hunting is better away from the roads.

captains Lewis and Clark spied the Highwoods and assumed they'd reached the threshold of the Rocky Mountains. Blackfeet Indians favored the little mountain range, not only for its summer shade, but for the elevated vantage point from which bison herds could be located far out on the prairie.

Though only about fifteen miles across, the Highwoods pop to an impressive seventy-five-hundred-plus feet above sea level. As expected, their sudden elevation gain yields some steep, rough terrain, most notably on the southern portion of the range. Like the Little Belts, the Highwoods are heavily forested, yielding superb escape cover for the trophy bull elk that track the highlands. All elk hunting in the Highwoods is by special permit only. Hunters enjoy good access to available public lands on the Lewis and Clark National Forest.

Elk Distribution

Elk inhabit most of the Little Belts, wintering in fairly specific areas in the foothills and the mountain flanks, then dispersing to higher ground in late spring. Analyze the wintering areas of elk and it's possible to gain some sense of where they're likely to roam come autumn.

On the northwest side of the range, elk winter in the lowlands just north of the National Forest boundary around Black Butte and Tiger Butte. Elk from the Black Butte area wander up the Deep Creek drainage and eastward toward Logging Creek, while the Tiger Butte herd splinters into small bands that head up Logging and Pilgrim creeks and to the east toward Bighorn and Monarch Mountains.

A good number of elk winter in the Otter Creek drainage east of Otter Mountain on the northeast side of the mountains. Elk also pass the snowy season in the bottoms along Lone Tree Creek a bit further east. By summer these animals are likely found toward the headwaters of the numerous tributaries of Belt Creek or the high ridges above Lone Tree Creek from Granite Mountain westward to the Anderson Peak vicinity.

The Judith River State Wildlife Management Area (JRWMA) lies adjacent to the national forest on the east side of the Little Belts. Elk winter on the WMA and private lands to the north around Mary's Knoll. Wapiti associated with this winter range move up the Lost Fork and Middle Fork of the Judith River to summer east of U.S. Highway 87. Look for them in the high country from the Judith River–Smith River divide on the southern portion of the range, north to highland haunts around Cabin Mountain and Teepee Butte. Elk also disperse up Yogo Creek toward its headwaters and the numerous peaks scattered on the lofty north-south ridge, which includes Elk Saddle and Tucker Mountain.

On the southeast side of the Little Belts, a mountainous spur extends some twenty miles eastward. Elk prefer the Antelope Creek drainage on the north side as a wintering area but scatter freely on the south side of the spur from the Roberts Creek drainage westward to the Haymaker State Wildlife Management Area. The greatest number of animals occurs on the Haymaker WMA and adjacent drainages to the west. Elk from these winter refuges populate the basins and ridges along the east-west-lying ridge that divides the Judith and Musselshell rivers during the summer.

A series of foothills connects the south side of the Little Belts with the north side of the Castle Mountains. Although interloping elk wander between the ranges, the lowlands along the North Fork of the Smith

River near Volcano Butte and Ice Creek are a favored wintering place for area elk. These animals roam the many high tributaries of the North Fork during the summer and fall but also drift further north and east.

On the west side of the Little Belts, traditional wintering grounds include the Black Butte Creek drainage northeast of Sheep Mountain and the foothills in the Strawberry Gulch–Blacktail Creek area just east of the Smith River. With the arrival of summer, these elk climb toward the headwaters of the many tributaries of Spring Creek west of U.S. Highway 89 from Mizpah Peak to Williams Mountain and further west in the Wood Mountain and Reynolds Mountain area.

In sum, elk in the Little Belts spread into nearly every nook and cranny of available habitat. Although distinct herds of a hundred or more animals tend to winter in the same area year after year, these animals disperse throughout the mountains in sometimes unpredictable patterns. Elk numbers tend to be somewhat higher on the southern and eastern portions of the range, but elk are found pretty much anywhere you care to look.

Where to Hunt

Little Belt Mountains

Although the Little Belts don't harbor the most elk in the state or boast what I would consider the most scenic destination, these mountains are one of the state's most popular hunting areas for a number of reasons. First, they're easily accessible from Great Falls, Billings, and Helena, three of Montana's major population centers. Second, they produce an abundant elk harvest, to the extent that a regional wildlife manager once described the Little Belts to me as an "elk factory." Finally, the mountains promote two very different hunting experiences that appeal to diverse segments of the population. On the one hand, easy vehicle access and numerous roads are found in many portions of this mountain range. However, several major roadless or travel-restricted areas also grace the landscape, offering a decidedly backcountry experience for solitude seekers.

The major route of public entry into the Little Belts occurs along Highway 89, which bisects the range from north to south. Additionally, county roads or other public access routes reach the Lewis and Clark National Forest at regular intervals around the mountains' perimeter. Although local hunters return to favored areas every season, MDFWP statistics indicate that both hunting pressure and elk harvest are spread fairly consistently throughout the several hunting districts that cover the range.

Hunters looking for easy vehicle access have numerous options in the Little Belts. On the south side of the range, Studhorse Road (FR 830) winds along Newlan Creek east of Highway 89, about three miles north of the Lewis and Clark National Forest boundary, some sixteen miles north of White Sulphur Springs. South of Studhorse Road is a small vehicle-restricted area. To the north, spur routes branch out toward several minor tributaries of the North Fork of the Smith River.

A bit further north, Sheep Creek Road (FR 119) departs Highway 89 to the west, then forks after about five miles near Moose Creek. Both Moose Creek Road (FR 204) and Sheep Creek Road offer easy vehicle access and camping. Vehicle-restricted roads and trails offer many options for hike-in hunting east of Moose Creek. Sheep Creek Road winds north, eventually topping Quartzite Ridge, which divides the Sheep Creek and Tenderfoot Creek drainages. South of the ridge several trails offer hunting via foot, horseback, or motorbike. It requires more hiking, but hunters that target the less-traveled areas between the trails find the best success.

At the summit of Quartzite Ridge, Sheep Creek Road meets FR 839, which runs northward from King's Hill Pass to Logging Creek Road south of Sluice Boxes State Park on the north side of the mountains. Numerous trails are found south and west of FR 839 in the Tenderfoot Creek drainage, most of which are open to motorbikes or ATVs. Some sizeable blocks of habitat fall between these motorized accessible trails, offering good hunting for those willing to park their machines and walk.

East of FR 839, those seeking a nonmotorized experience might check out the area between Logging and Pilgrim creeks, which is generally free of roads and trails. Access to this area is easiest from the north side of the mountains. About two miles north of the national forest boundary on Highway 89, take Logging Creek Road west for about ten miles. It then turns south along Logging Creek and heads toward the interior of the mountains.

Motorized access is also plentiful on the northeast side of the Little Belts from several routes. From Highway 89, FR 120 runs east from Monarch along the Dry Fork of Belt Creek, leading beyond the old mining communities of Barker and Hughesville to connect with FR 251, which eventually intersects U.S. Highway 87 near Stanford. Several spur roads and trails, which are open to motorbikes, branch from FR 120. Although the tendency among most hunters is to head toward the end of the road, in the late season hunting can actually be better lower down if there's enough snow to bump elk from higher elevations.

Another venue for vehicle-based hunting includes the corridor of roads and trails that extends from the east side of the mountains between the Lost Fork and South Fork of the Judith River to the North Fork of the Musselshell River and Spring Creek on the south side of the Little Belts. To reach this area from the east, take State Highway 239 west of Hobson from Highway 87 to Utica (nine miles). At Utica, veer southwest onto County Road 1 (Judith River Road), which becomes FR 487 when it enters the Lewis and Clark National Forest about fifteen miles from Utica. Numerous roads and trails stem from FR 487 between the Lost Fork and South Fork of the Judith River; many of these are closed to all vehicle travel during elk season but offer easy hiking to more remote habitat. Some nineteen miles from the national forest boundary, FR 487 swings to the northwest, eventually intersecting Highway 89 at King's Hill. Hunting prospects abound along 487, including the area east of Dry Pole Canyon, which sometimes holds good numbers of elk toward the end of the hunting season.

From the south, abundant motorized access awaits hunters from FR 274 at Spring Creek. FR 274 heads north from U.S. Highway 12 about twenty-three miles east of White Sulphur Springs. Roughly eighteen miles from Highway 12, it intersects FR 487. Many branch roads and trails depart from 274 in the Spring Creek drainage, offering plentiful hunting opportunities within walking distance of a vehicle.

East of the Spring Creek area, several motorized access routes enter the Little Belts on the southeast side of the range. County Road 101 (RD 12W88N) runs north of Highway 12 at Two Dot. About seven miles from Highway 12, look for County Road 121 (RD 12W88NA), which departs west of 121. This route leads to Haymaker WMA and the national forest. Once in the national forest several vehicle routes lead north and others east, providing good access to the southeastern spur of mountains that extends from the central portion of the Little Belts to the east. Expect the best hunting in the hikeable areas between the vehicle routes.

Motorized users tend to hold the upper hand in the Lewis and Clark National Forest in the Little Belts, but several excellent destinations for backcountry hunting exist as well. On the southeastern side of the mountains, a fair-size chunk of roadless and vehicle-restricted real estate lies south of FR 487 toward the South Fork of the Judith River and its tributaries, from Dry Pole Canyon on the east to Deadhorse Creek on the west. Hike trail 439 along the South Fork of the Judith River from FR 487 or head cross-country from the road.

Several miles north, an expansive block of roadless country sprawls across the east-central portion of the Little Belts in the Middle Fork of the Judith River drainage. Currently, some trails in this drainage are open to motorbikes during archery season but aren't allowed from October 15 to December 1, eliminating all motorized travel during the general season. Hiking or horseback entry is possible from several locations, including FR 487 south of King's Hill and FR 251 to the north. However, trails from these two routes tend to run downhill, making for an uphill climb at the end of the day. From the east, trails lead up the drainage, which makes for easier walking on the return trip. FR 825 follows the Middle Fork of the Judith River (see previous driving directions to FR 487 from Utica to reach 825, which branches west just before the national forest boundary). From FR 825, take any of several trails that head north and south, or strike out directly from the road.

Table 9-1 Little Belt Mountains

	Low	Moderate	High	Very High
Elk Numbers		●		
Hunters Per Square Mile				●
Hunters Per Elk				●
Trophy Potential	●			
Remote/Roadless Areas		●		

North of the Judith River's Middle Fork, a couple of smaller motorized-restricted and roadless areas are found in the Yogo Creek and Dry Wolf Creek drainages. To reach the Yogo Creek region, take Yogo Creek Road (FR 266) west of the Judith River Road about eleven miles west of Utica. Several vehicle-restricted routes run north of FR 266, and a sizeable chunk of roadless land also spreads to the south toward Kelly Mountain and Woodchopper Ridge. Currently, a portion of HD 420 lies northwest of Yogo Creek, where elk hunting is restricted to a special permit, so check your hunting regulations carefully before trekking into that area.

To reach the Dry Wolf Creek drainage, take County Road 101 (FR 251) south from Highway 87 just west of Stanford. Some twenty miles from Highway 87 watch for trail 401 near the Dry Wolf Campground. This trail and its branches are closed to motorbikes after October 15, as is trail 416 to the west, which runs along the divide between Dry Wolf Creek and the Dry Fork of Belt Creek. These seasonal closures yield a considerable expanse of country on the west side of Dry Wolf Creek that's only open to nonmotorized travel during the general elk season. Use the available trails, but also look for elk tucked away in remote basins and seldom-traveled ridges.

Highwood Mountains

Although they're an isolated mountain range ringed in private land, public access for elk hunting in the Highwood Mountains is more than adequate, provided you're willing to do some hiking. FR 121 essentially bisects the range from north to south, with a few branch roads fanning east and west from this main route. To reach FR 121, motor up State Highway 228 (Highwood Road) east of Great Falls. About a mile south of Highwood, watch for County Road 200, which becomes FR 121 upon its entry to the Lewis and Clark National Forest some fourteen miles from Highway 228. Several trails branch out from around the Thain Creek Campground west of FR 121. Presently, these trails are open to motorbikes until October 15 but are closed to all motorized travel during the general elk season.

Hunting district 447, which encompasses the Highwood Mountains, is currently open to either-sex elk hunting during the archery season on a

Table 9-2 Highwood Mountains

	Low	Moderate	High	Very High
Elk Numbers		●		
Hunters Per Square Mile		●		
Hunters Per Elk			●	
Trophy Potential^				●
Remote/Roadless Areas		●		

^ Special tag required for general season.

general elk license. Youths ages 12 through 15 may take an antlerless animal on a general license during general season, but all other rifle elk hunting requires a special permit. The Highwoods have a deserved reputation for trophy bulls—provided you luck into an either-sex tag in the drawing. Current odds for resident hunters are about one in fifteen. In addition to those in the national forest, limited opportunities may be available for elk hunting on block management properties.

Hunting Strategies

Both the Little Belt and Highwood mountains are quite heavily timbered, except for scattered open parks and areas cleared by logging or fire. Although many hunters like to cruise the roads in a pickup or steer a motorbike up the trails hoping to catch elk in the open, those who penetrate the timber find better success. Given the plentiful amount of wapiti tracking the pines and the liberal hunting regulations in the Little Belts (general-license hunting for any antlered bull for the entire general season and either-sex hunting for a portion of the season), patient sneaking through the timber should give any competent hunter a shot at an elk. Even if the herd bests you in the "I spy" game four out of five times, you'll still down a Little Belt elk, providing you're persistent.

Hunt the edges of forest at dawn and dusk, as animals will likely be moving to and from these areas to feed. Although elk often retreat well away from motorized travel routes, it doesn't always take a Herculean hike

There's always a good place to hunt in the Little Belts—up high when it's hot, lower down when there's snow.

to find them. Where a road winds along a slope just a half-mile from a ridgetop, you'll often find elk bedded on the summit.

In many Montana locations, hunting very early in the season is almost essential to catch elk on public land before they're pushed onto private. Throughout most of the Little Belts, a notable percentage of animals typically stays in the national forest until the end of hunting season and beyond. As a general strategy, hunt higher elevations and the interior of the mountains during the early part of the season. Later on, especially if there's significant snowfall, look for animals at lower elevations, particularly in those areas adjacent to the traditional wintering grounds described earlier in this chapter.

10

BIG BELT,
ELKHORN MOUNTAINS

----------◆----------

Geographical Overview

In many respects the Elkhorn and Big Belt mountains of central Montana are similar. Both are rather arid, receiving considerably less precipitation than many other ranges in the state. Precious metals brought nineteenth-century miners into the bowels of each massif, prospecting for gold, silver, and copper. Their pinnacles also rise to similar heights: Mount Edith is the highest point in the Big Belts at 9,504 feet above sea level; Crow Peak, the loftiest summit in the Elkhorns, rises to 9,414 feet.

Both ranges boast superb elk habitat, though the Elkhorns get the nod in that category. Many biologists believe the Elkhorns represent *the* finest elk country in the state. Sufficient grass and forage sprouts each spring to keep wapiti well fed during the summer, while low snowpack and productive winter range promotes excellent calf survival and reproduction.

Not only are the Elkhorns friendly toward elk, they're equally hospitable to hunters. Several steep peaks cluster in the southern part of the range around Crow Peak, with a similar scattering on the north side in the High Peak vicinity. Elsewhere, the terrain is moderately pitched, making it quite easy to hike and hunt. The Helena National Forest sprawls over most of the range, with numerous access sites available from all points of the compass. Due to a special directive, the portion of the Helena National Forest in the Elkhorn Range is managed as a Wildlife

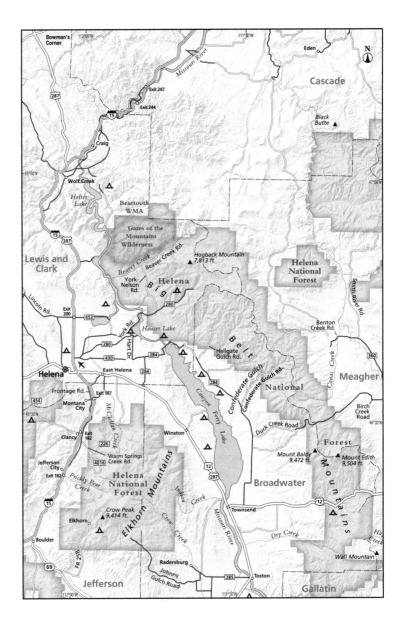

Management Unit, the only one of its kind in the National Forest System. Since 1986 a major objective within the unit is to "optimize elk winter range" and evaluate other uses against this overarching goal.

Though very productive elk habitat, the Elkhorns aren't a particularly large range. Lying southeast of Helena, the mountains run about thirty miles north to south and twenty miles from east to west. Generally speaking, the south and west portions have less timber cover. The north and east sides are more heavily forested, but the evergreens are broken by scattered parks and open hillsides where elk are more visible to hunters.

At eighty miles from north to south and fifteen miles or less from east to west, the Big Belts run from the north end of the Bridger Range to the Gates of the Mountains area along the Missouri River near Helena. These mountains are somewhat steeper overall than the Elkhorns but are still easily traversed by hunters in most places. As one travels from south to north, the terrain becomes noticeably more rugged, culminating in the Gates of the Mountains Wilderness Area. Among the smallest designated wildernesses in Montana, the Gates of the Mountains covers some 28,500 acres. This is rough, rugged country, dominated by sharply canted ridges covered with timber and sheer limestone battlements that flank the ridgetops and plunge into deep, shady ravines.

Like the Elkhorns, the Big Belts are dominated by public land administered by the Helena National Forest. Access for hunting abounds, though private lands on the southern end of the range pose some limitations.

Isolated meadows, like this one in the Elkhorn Mountains, may be the feeding grounds of a tremendous bull.

Elk Distribution

It's safe to say that within the Elkhorn Mountains elk occupy essentially all habitat they find to their liking, which pretty much characterizes the entire range. Rather than describe the areas where elk abound, it's easier to note where they're absent.

Elk tolerate steep, heavily timbered terrain but also need some open areas or breaks in the forest canopy that promote the growth of grasses, shrubs, and succulent plants for food. Most of the Elkhorn range provides wapiti with this essential mix, but some areas, like the steep, heavily forested, rocky slopes around Crow Peak and Elkhorn Peak, aren't regularly frequented by elk. Additionally, elk typically move away from vehicle disturbance along roads and human activity along heavily used trails. Other than the previously mentioned areas, some two thousand head of elk (give or take a few hundred) scatter across the Elkhorns during the summer. Biologists with the MDFWP estimate that about 90 percent of the elk in HD 380, which includes the Elkhorns, summer on public lands administered by the state, the Forest Service, and the BLM. Compared to most other central mountain ranges where the vast majority of elk winter on private land, roughly 70 percent of the animals in HD 380 remain on public acreage throughout the winter.

As do animals in the Elkhorns, wapiti scatter across almost the entire expanse of the Big Belt Mountains during summer months, with the exception of the steep, rocky slopes and areas of highest elevation. From the elevated ridges and basins, they move to the foothills to winter. On the southern and central segments of the range, much of their wintering grounds occur on private land. On the northern end, though, numerous animals utilize the Beartooth Wildlife Management Area east of Holter Lake and scattered sections of state and BLM lands that are interspersed with private lands between the Missouri and Shields rivers.

The south side of the Big Belts extends almost to the Bridger Mountains. The southern foothills of the Big Belts in the Sixteenmile Creek drainage, which separates the Bridgers and Big Belts, is highly productive elk country. Wapiti are plentiful in the Sixteenmile Creek area, scattered from Wall Mountain on the east side of the range westward to the hills just east of Toston. Further north, good numbers are found from the upper reaches of Dry Creek on the west side of the range and Hay Creek on the east side of the range to Confederate Gulch on the west side and Camas Creek on the east side.

Similarly, elk occupy both the east and west side of the Big Belts from Camas Creek and Confederate Gulch all the way to the northern end of the range in the Wolf Creek area. Just west of the Smith River south of Rock Creek, the Dry Range is an isolated, mountainous area east of the Big Belts. A few sections of national forest land are found in the Dry Range, but adjacent private lands buffer them from public hunting.

North of the Beartooth Wildlife Management Area on the north end of the Big Belts, a small region of steep mountains rises from the eastern banks of the Missouri River. Elk track the canted ridges in this area, which appears on the map as a haphazard mixture of private, BLM, and state land. Elk are also scattered in the hills east of this region to the breaks along Smith River. Most of this land is privately owned or exists in isolated pieces of public land surrounded by private holdings. However, landowner cooperation with hunters is quite good in this area, with a number of block management properties available.

Where to Hunt

Elkhorn Mountains

The Elkhorn Mountains boast excellent hunting with many points of access. However, regulations in HD 380 impose limitations on the harvest of brow-tined bulls to tags issued in a drawing. On a general license, hunters may only take spike bulls, bulls "having antlers which do not branch, or if branched, the branch is less than four inches long measured from the main antler." The taking of antlerless elk is also restricted to draw-only tags, but good odds and easy hunting make these tags popular with area hunters. Either-sex tags that allow the killing of a brow-tined bull are extremely hard to secure, with less than 2 percent of the applicants pulling a tag. However, the average age of bulls taken on these either-sex tags usually exceeds five years, yielding many, many exceptional animals.

On the east side of the range, two major access routes leave from Radersburg, a once-booming but now tiny mining community in the southeastern foothills. To reach Radersburg, take State Highway 285 west from U.S. Highway 287 just south of the Missouri River near Toston. It's about eight miles to Radersburg.

A little before reaching Radersburg, watch for Johnny Gulch Road. This route (FR 621) ambles west, then turns north before reaching the boundary of the Helena National Forest after some thirteen miles. Prior to entering the national forest, the road winds through several sections of BLM land, which may hold elk. Once in the national forest, elk can be encountered in any direction.

North of Radersburg, Crow Creek Road (FR 424) provides access to much of the southeastern portion of the Elkhorns, either from the road itself or from spur routes that branch out to other locations. Several campgrounds perch along the road, offering multiple options for pitching a hunting camp. I've spotted elk from my vehicle numerous times from Crow Creek Road, most often at the edges of the timbered slopes. Near the end of the road, trail 110 offers travel via foot or horseback into a roadless area to the west—look here for good hunting in a more backcountry setting.

For access to the northeast side of the Elkhorns, Indian Creek Road, just a mile north of Townsend, west of Highway 287, represents an excellent option. This route hits the national forest boundary about ten miles from the highway but passes through BLM land on the way. Once in the national forest, good hunting opportunities abound.

Not too far up Highway 287 from Indian Creek, public passage to the Elkhorns is also available from Weasel Creek Road (FR 405). Twelve miles north of Townsend, this road launches west of the highway at Winston. From the highway it's about five miles to the entrance of the national forest. From the boundary, FR 405 runs several more miles to the head of Kimber Gulch. To the north and south, fairly steep country greets the hunter, but easier hiking awaits to the southwest.

On the northern front McClellan Creek Road (FR 226) offers a straight southern shot into the Elkhorns. From I-15 south of Helena, take exit 187 east onto State Highway 518. Just past the exit, look for McClellan Creek Road on the south side of the highway. It's about a

Early morning on the Iron Mask.

Elk and the Iron Mask

Not far from Indian Creek Road's entry to the Helena National Forest west of Townsend, elk hunters freely scour the timbered pockets and open ridges on the east front of the Elkhorns. Prior to 2005, though, the 5,550-acre property was held in private hands.

Thanks to the foresight of the Rocky Mountain Elk Foundation (RMEF), this sprawling tract of year-round elk habitat and crucial winter range wasn't lost to housing developments. When the Iron Mask property (named for the historic mining claim on its southwest corner) came up for sale in 2002, a local elk foundation volunteer spearheaded the effort to secure the land for elk—and elk hunters. After three tense years of negotiations and innovative solutions to seemingly insurmountable financial and logistical obstacles, the Rocky Mountain Elk Foundation closed the sale.

As an organization in the elk-habitat business, not land management, the Elk Foundation won't oversee the property. Instead the BLM will take the reins, with the express objective of maintaining and enhancing winter range. In September 2005 I witnessed firsthand that which the RMEF secured for the public. When I arrived at daylight, a heavy fog bank shrouded the hills, lending a ghostly aura to junipers and twisted limber pines that appeared as phantoms in a swirling fog. On assignment to photograph the property, I hiked toward a ridgetop, waiting for the warming rays of the morning sun to burn away the mist.

Near the summit, I noticed a tiny sliver of blue in the gray above. Other creatures also sensed the breaking dawn. From the ravine below, the wild, guttural blast of a bugling bull sliced the fog, loud and eerie in the stillness. Moments later, the sun broke through, raising the ashen curtain from the landscape, a beautiful tapestry of moss-covered stones, yellowed grass, aromatic sagebrush, and emerald evergreens. Though I recorded some fine landscape images, the photos stored on film seem a tawdry representation of those seared forever in my memory.

If you doubt the effectiveness of conservation organizations like the Rocky Mountain Elk Foundation, all the logic and literature in the world isn't apt to change your mind. But let me offer an additional avenue of persuasion. On a fine fall morning, when yellow cottonwoods light the ravines and dark-maned bulls bugle on the hillsides, visit the Iron Mask. Contemplate the landscape. Imagine it dotted with a hundred houses, absent of elk. Hear the barking dogs, the slamming doors, and the clatter of internal combustion engines.

Humans need homes. But elk do, too. Conservation organizations that secure habitat preserve not only the lives of wild creatures but the spirits of humans as well.

four-mile drive to the Helena National Forest boundary. Several roads branch from this main artery, along with a couple of foot trails. Hunt the lowlands later in the season, or if it's hot, scour the more elevated slopes in the Casey and High Peak vicinity. If you hunt this area, be aware that a major fire scorched a huge expanse of country a couple of decades ago. Fallen timber mingled with new growth from small pine trees makes foot travel very difficult in places.

From the west, look for good public access at Prickly Pear Creek via FR 164. From I-15 about thirteen miles north of Boulder, take exit 176. Just east of the interstate, turn south and head toward the Prickly Pear Creek drainage. This route makes a nine-mile climb to the east-west divide of the mountains, with a number of spur routes fanning from the main road. The Manley Park area toward the end of the road is popular with elk hunters, but early pressure often moves animals away from this well-used destination. However tempting the roads, this is an excellent place to burn your boot soles. Elk are found in all directions but are most plentiful away from the noise and commotion close to the roads.

Elkhorn, a once-booming mining town bustling with thousands of human bodies, now stands nearly deserted within the national forest on the south side of the Elkhorn Range. Two routes lead to Elkhorn via FR 258. One heads east of State Highway 69 about two miles south of Boulder (watch for the signs to Elkhorn). The other also runs east of Highway 69 but is found about fourteen miles south of Boulder. Like other major access routes into the Elkhorns, narrower vehicle trails branch from FR

Table 10-1 Elkhorn Mountains

	Low	Moderate	High	Very High
Elk Numbers			●	
Hunters Per Square Mile				●
Hunters Per Elk			●	
Trophy Potential^				●
Remote/Roadless Areas		●		

^ Special tag required.

258, along with several hiking trails. Trails 74 and 128 on the west side of the road provide access to the headwaters of McCarty Creek and Rawhide Creek on the west flank of the mountains, yielding a more back-country setting for elk hunting than areas adjacent to the road. Beyond the town of Elkhorn, FR 258 and its branches become very rough and impassable with much snow cover. In addition to national forest lands, elk are sometimes found on tracts of BLM ground via FR 517 east of Elkhorn Creek adjacent to the national forest and similar state lands a mile or so to the west. Access these by hiking from the national forest to avoid trespassing on private land.

Big Belt Mountains

Much of the southern end of the Big Belt Mountains, while excellent elk habitat, is found on private land or small parcels of public land, making hunting a very uncertain proposition. U.S. Highway 12 runs from Townsend, east across the mountains, with some public access to the south. About seventeen miles east of Townsend, Sulphur Bar Road (FR 147) provides access to the headwaters of Sulphur Bar and Cedar Bar creeks. Hunting is possible in this area, but attend carefully to property boundaries, as it's easy to stray onto private land to the south and west. Like many other small public areas, hunting pressure here in the first days of the season typically bumps elk from public land to private.

North of Highway 12, less than a mile west of Sulphur Bar Road, Cabin Gulch Road (FR 423) snakes north into the heart of the southern Big Belts. The road then loops back west and finally south, reconnecting with Highway 12 along the North Fork of Deep Creek. Several minor roads branch from this route, as do a handful of hiking trails. Trails 107 and 152 depart from the north portion of this loop road, offering access by foot or horseback to the high, steep slopes south of Mount Edith. Look for the best hunting in isolated pockets, small basins, and remote ridges.

Moving north, the next point of easy public access to the Big Belts is found from Birch Creek/Duck Creek Road (FR 139), which crosses the mountains from east to west. On the east side of the range, Birch Creek Road departs from State Highway 360, about two miles west of White

Sulphur Springs. Some thirteen miles west, the road enters the Helena National Forest near the Gipsy Lake campground. From the west, Duck Creek Road branches from State Highway 284 on the east side of Canyon Ferry Lake about thirteen miles north of Townsend. From the highway, a drive of around nine miles leads to the national forest. From the top of Duck Creek Pass, trails depart to the north and south. This is high, beautiful country, much of it reserved for nonmotorized travel. To the southeast, there's prime elk habitat in the headwaters of Birch and Little Birch creeks. Take trail 151 from the top of the pass or trail 150 at the Gipsy Lake Campground to reach this area. North of the pass, steep terrain awaits on the west side of the divide, but good elk country that's easier to travel is found on the upper slopes of the Camas Creek drainage.

Roughly four miles north of Duck Creek Road on Highway 284 on the west side of the mountains, the Confederate Gulch Road (FR 287) winds its way across the range, connecting with Highway 360 not far from the Smith River. Hunting is possible from this road in both directions,

The Big Belt Mountains aren't known as a trophy area, but better-than-average bulls roam the northern end of range.

Table 10-2 Big Belt Mountains

	Low	Moderate	High	Very High
Elk Numbers			●	
Hunters Per Square Mile				●
Hunters Per Elk		●		
Trophy Potential^	●			
Remote/Roadless Areas	●			

^ High in north end of the mountains (HD 455). Special tag required in general season.

though the country east of the route above the abandoned Diamond City is more insulated from human disturbance.

From the west side of the Big Belts, several access points to public land originate in the area around the Canyon Ferry Dam. Magpie Creek Road (FR 425) is one option; look for it about three miles east of Canyon Ferry on State Highway 284. Just north of Canyon Ferry, Jimtown Road (FR 231) connects with York/Trout Creek Road to the north. Both Jimtown and Magpie Creek roads offer fine access to the lower slopes of the mountains, with the Magpie Creek route eventually leading to the top of the Missouri and Smith river divide. Look for elk at low elevations in this area later in the fall; scour the high country during archery season and toward the beginning of the general season.

Further north, State Highway 280 runs west of Helena and into the Helena National Forest east of the Missouri River. Also known as York Road, this route weaves along Trout Creek in the Trout Creek Canyon. A better bet for elk hunting is found at York-Nelson Road (RD 4) which branches north of York Road just two miles beyond the boundary to the national forest. About eight miles beyond its junction with York Road, the York-Nelson Road terminates at Beaver Creek Road (FR 138), which winds southeast along Beaver Creek, then loops back to the south not far from Hogback Mountain. Northwest of the Beaver Creek Road lies the Gates of the Mountains Wilderness Area, where elk graze the high meadows and range high among the pines. The northern portion of this wilderness area and the adjacent Beartooth Wildlife Management Area compose HD 455, where the harvest of bull elk during the rifle season is restricted to those holding a special tag—physically demanding country but a good place to find a trophy.

Hunting Strategies

As elk are scattered throughout both mountain ranges covered in this chapter, any hunter willing to work promising habitat, especially that away from the roads, has good prospects for success. In the Big Belts the greatest portion of the annual elk harvest, especially bulls, occurs early in the general season before animals are pushed from public to private lands.

North and east of the Big Belts, HD 445 lies outside what some would consider traditional elk habitat, though a robust population of wapiti roams this area. Although private land dominates HD 445, access to these lands for elk hunting is much better than most places in the state. A number of block management properties allow easy public access, while some local landowners not enrolled in block management also grant permission for elk hunting. Currently, bull harvest is limited to general tag holders for just the first two weeks of the season or to those holding a special either-sex tag good for the entire season. If you utilize private land in this HD, extend every courtesy to the benevolent landowners who host hunters on private land.

In the Elkhorns special regulations governing elk hunting lend themselves to particular hunting strategies. As general tags are only good for spike bull elk, hunters looking to down one of these fine-eating yearling males should hunt the cow herds. Unlike older bulls that usually break from the females to form their own small bachelor herds after the rut, spikes often stick with the cow herds through the winter. Where you find cows, you'll generally locate spikes, especially during the early part of the season.

With the exceedingly long odds of drawing a tag, most assume that dropping a brow-tined bull on an either-sex tag in the Elkhorns is easy. It isn't. Although a much higher percentage of older bulls exists in the population, the number of males in the post-season population (spikes included) only numbers about 10 percent of the elk herd. What's more, these older bulls have survived numerous hunting seasons, making them an exceptionally wily quarry. As soon as the general season opens, hunting pressure pushes them into timber and the most remote portions of the mountains. A number of years ago I pulled one of these coveted tags. I spotted two excellent bulls opening morning but couldn't get in position to shoot. Though I hunted hard for more than a week during the remainder of the season, my tag remained unfilled when the cold November dusk expired the Sunday after Thanksgiving. Just because you luck into an HD 380 either-sex tag, don't assume that the big bull is in the bag.

11

WESTERN MISSOURI BREAKS, JUDITH MOUNTAINS, SWEETGRASS HILLS

------------◆------------

Geographical Overview

North-central Montana consists primarily of flat or rolling prairie. Historically covered in native grass and shrubs, much of the area now produces agricultural crops such as wheat, barley, and alfalfa hay. Cattle ranching is also prevalent in the area, with bovines grazing both native grasslands and tilled fields of pasture, improved via the introduction of alfalfa or grasses that produce more forage than native varieties.

Disruptions to these softer features of the landscape occur in isolated mountain ranges that seemingly pop from the prairie with no apparent pattern. Twisted breaks, dotted with evergreens, also provide relief along the Missouri River, though their presence and severity fades as one moves westward up the river.

In the southern portion of this region, the Judith Mountains spring from the prairie north of Lewistown. The Judiths are a tiny range by Montana standards; from east to west and north to south, their breadth scarcely extends beyond twelve miles in any direction. Though their elevation is low by Rocky Mountain standards (under six thousand feet), these mountains are nevertheless heavily timbered, providing good escape cover for elk.

North of the Judith Mountains, the Upper Missouri Breaks National Monument sprawls across lands adjacent to the river. Almost directly north of the Judith Mountains, the east-flowing Missouri River abruptly swings south in a series of

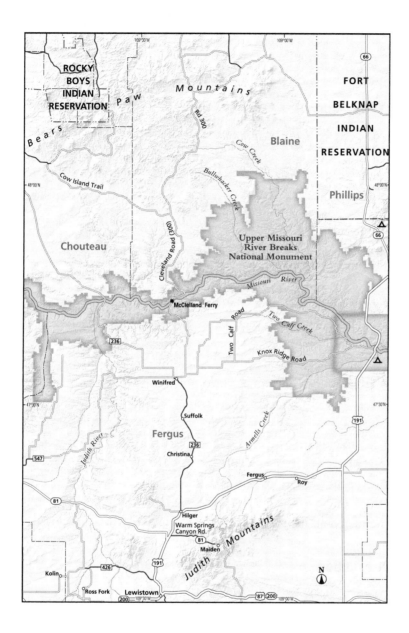

looping bends, before returning to its eastward course. This variation in the river's course also marks a fairly significant change in area topography. To the west, the breaks along the river aren't nearly as rugged as those found to the east, although enough timber cover and contour still exists to harbor elk.

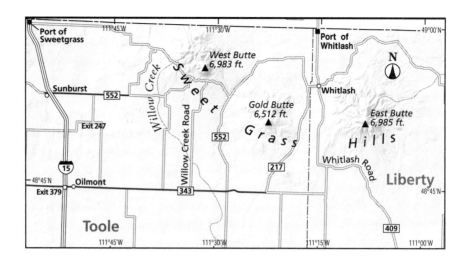

Northwest of this area, the Bears Paw Mountains rise above the plains south of Havre. Several peaks rise more than six thousand feet above sea level, and Baldy Mountain on the southern end of the range nears seven thousand. Like the Judiths, the slopes of these mountains nourish thick stands of timber, which provide cover for elk.

Just south of the Canadian border, the Sweetgrass Hills thrust abruptly from the landscape in a series of buttes northeast of Shelby. These are fascinatingly beautiful mountains that tower a full three thousand feet above the surrounding pastures and farmland. There's enough forest cover on the various buttes to shelter elk, though apparently some don't think much of the area. A young, radio-collared bull from this area once wandered all the way to the state of Missouri.

Elk Distribution

Several hundred elk range in the Judith Mountain vicinity. Summer finds them at higher elevations within the mountains, dropping to lower elevations during the late fall and winter. Large numbers of area elk inhabit the northeast portion of the Judith Mountains in the fall, where they find sanctuary from hunters on a few large ranches.

In the Upper Missouri Breaks area, elk distribution occurs in a pattern similar to that further down the river. Most elk hang within a few miles of the river in the timbered breaks but occupy other parcels of suitable habitat further north and south. In the eastern portion of this area, good habitat is found in the rough country along Armells Creek and Two Calf Creek on the south side of the river and in the Antelope Creek area on the north side. A bit further west, elk roam the fairly expansive Cow Creek and Bullwhacker Creek drainages north of the Missouri River, west to the Lion Coulee region. West of the confluence of the Judith and Missouri rivers, elk habitat, and numbers, are limited by topography and agricultural production.

To the north, in the Sweetgrass Hills, elk commonly use higher-elevation areas of Douglas fir and lodgepole pine forests for shade and security but also spread out onto adjacent land, which mostly consists of dryland grain farms and native or tilled pasture for cattle. Sweetgrass Hills elk interchange with herds found in southern Alberta and Saskatchewan, Canada. This movement predominates among bulls whose unpredictable border hopping has been well documented by wildlife researchers.

Expect fairly low elk numbers and scattered herds in the western Missouri Breaks. You'll need to get out and hike to find them.

Where to Hunt

There's fine elk hunting in the Judith Mountains, but access for public hunting is difficult. State Highway 81 (Maiden Road) runs east of U.S. Highway 191 about ten miles north of Lewistown into the Judiths. Some ten miles east of Highway 191, the route enters BLM land, then branches north and south, giving fairly easy access to public land in the central portion of the range. Energetic hunters who are handy with a map can also pick their way east and west onto staggered chunks of state and BLM land that mingle with private. However, hunting seasons, both archery and general, find most elk on private land. Throughout this area, only one in five elk killed by hunters falls on public acreage. Current regulations in HD 412 allow hunting for either-sex elk by archers, but all general-season hunting requires a special elk permit.

In the upper Missouri Breaks region, hunting access is much easier. Several public roads lead to public land, with high participation in the block management program occurring among private landowners both north and south of the Missouri River. Like other districts in the Missouri Breaks, elk hunting in these areas requires a special permit.

West of Highway 191, north and south of its crossing of the "Mighty Mo" at the Fred Robinson Bridge, entry to the Charles M. Russell NWR is possible for public hunting. On the south side of the river, access to the Armells Creek and Two Calf Creek areas is also possible by traveling east from State Highway 236 at Winifred. Look for Two Calf Road on the east side of Winifred. About eleven miles east, this route turns north for roughly five miles, then heads back east toward public land along the Missouri River. Another route, the Knox Ridge Road, continues east toward Armells and Two Calf creeks, yielding access to public lands in this area, which offer good hunting.

Entry to BLM lands on the north side of the Missouri River is also possible from the Winifred area through the archery season and the early portion of the general season. Head east of Winifred on Two Calf Road, then watch for the road (and signs), which turns north toward the McClelland Ferry. This ferry provides seasonal crossings of the Missouri River from April through October. North of the ferry, Cleveland Road (FR 300) provides access to public lands along the river. Some eighteen

A fine bull in typical habitat in the prairie country of central Montana.

miles north of the ferry, Cow Island Trail runs east and west, offering a driving route to public lands in the Bullwhacker Creek drainage. After the ferry closes for the season, look for access to this area from State Highway 240, which runs south of U.S. Highway 2 at Chinook. About twenty-five miles from Chinook, look for Cleveland Road (300), which runs west around ten miles, then veers south for about thirty miles before intersecting Cow Island Trail. Access to the area is also possible from the west via Warrick Road, which heads east of State Highway 236 about two miles south of Big Sandy. Roughly sixteen miles east of Highway 236, Cow Island Trail veers south from Warrick Road, then swings back east for another thirty miles or so before entering the Bullwhacker area. Elk are scattered in the Bullwhacker area and to the northwest in the Bears Paw Mountains. Cooperation with hunters by private landowners is good through the block management program. Although overall numbers are fairly low, some big bulls inhabit this region.

The Sweet Grass Hills are an intriguing place to hunt elk in a unique setting. Though access to public lands can be difficult, landowner cooperation with the MDFWP for elk management and hunter access is excellent. Currently, several large block management areas allow very good opportunity for elk hunting on private land and adjacent public acreages.

Three distinct geological features compose the Sweetgrass Hills: West, Gold, and East buttes, with a few smaller buttes sprinkled around the area as well. East and West buttes are the largest mountainous areas, with the smaller Gold Butte located between. Wapiti move between the major habitats around East and West buttes, with numbers distributed equally between the two areas. Elk hunting in the Sweetgrass Hills (HD 401) requires a special permit, with fairly long odds of drawing an either-sex tag.

Vehicle access to the area is easy to find. From I-15, Oilmont Highway (State Highway 343) runs east at exit 379, fifteen miles north of Shelby. From this route, several good roads head north to the Sweetgrass Hills. Suphellen and Willow Creek roads provide access to the West Butte area, ten to fifteen miles east of I-15. Another seventeen miles or so beyond these routes, Whitlash Road runs north to the East Butte area. No matter how you access the Sweetgrass Hills, check with the MDFWP Region 4 office for up-to-date elk-hunting and block management information.

Table 11-1 Upper Missouri Breaks

	Low	Moderate	High	Very High
Elk Numbers		●		
Hunters Per Square Mile	●			
Hunters Per Elk	●			
Trophy Potential^			●	
Remote/Roadless Areas	●			

^ Special tag required in general season.

Table 11-2 Sweetgrass Hills

	Low	Moderate	High	Very High
Elk Numbers*	●			
Hunters Per Square Mile	●			
Hunters Per Elk	●			
Trophy Potential^			●	
Remote/Roadless Areas	●			

* Locally higher in good habitat.
^ Special tag required in general season. Public access may be difficult.

Hunting Strategies

In the Judith Mountains, hunting away from the roads to penetrate public lands adjacent to private is one probable avenue for success. Look for small bands of elk and lone bulls, moving very carefully so that you don't inadvertently spook your quarry onto land you can't access. Hunting pressure always peaks during the first week of the season, then typically spikes again during the last week. When pressure wanes toward the middle of the season, elk sometimes wander back onto public lands from private. Try this time period if you're intent on hunting the Judiths.

One of the keys to good elk hunting in the western Missouri Breaks and the Sweetgrass Hills is doing the required research to see what hunter access is available to private lands. This means obtaining block management maps and information from the appropriate regional office of MDFWP, but a call to inquire about nonformalized opportunities on private land is a good idea as well. Given the dispersed nature of elk herds in the upper Missouri Breaks, plan to do lots of glassing and hiking to find your quarry. Elk hunting in the Sweetgrass Hills is something of a casual affair to many hunters, involving lots of time in the cab of a pickup or on the seat of a four-wheeler. These folks find elk, but if you're searching for an exceptional bull, look for places the animals are buffered from vehicle disturbance and sneak in on foot.

12

GALLATIN RANGE,
MADISON RANGE

----------◆----------

Geographical Overview

From a historical standpoint, the Gallatin and Madison mountain ranges in south-west Montana are intimately linked with one of the most phenomenal feats of exploration on this continent, the Lewis and Clark expedition, or, as Thomas Jefferson named it, the Corps of Discovery. Of the several objectives given to the corps, locating the headwaters of the Missouri River and appraising their potential for navigation ranked high on the list. At Three Forks, under a warm July sun in 1805, the captains discovered the three tributaries that form the Missouri River, describing the site as "an essential point in the geography of this western part of the continent."

Two of these streams take most of their water from the Madison and Gallatin ranges, which bear the same names as the rivers that drain them. Of the two ranges, the Madison is higher. Six summits rise in excess of eleven thousand feet with another 120 or so topping ten thousand feet, making the Madison Range the second highest in Montana. On the east side the mountains are bounded by the Gallatin River. South of the resort community of Big Sky and the Gallatin Canyon, the Gallatin River valley broadens in a meadow-type environment, which is critical wintering ground for elk and other big-game species. Despite the numerous steep, high peaks, much of the Madison Range consists of verdant, grassy meadows and winsome alpine basins that recline below imposing crags. Unlike many mountain ranges whose summits fall along a well-defined ridge, the Madison's peaks are

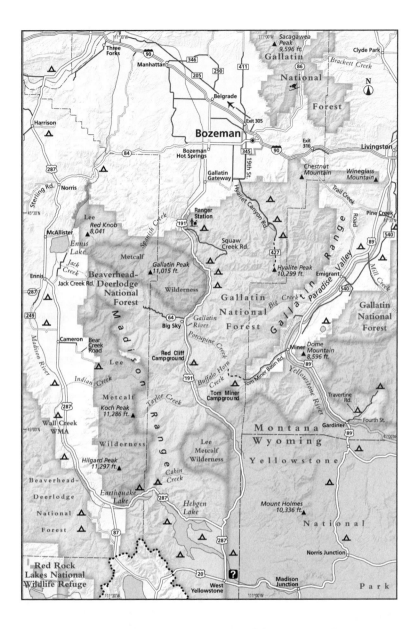

clustered haphazardly throughout the range. The western front is particularly steep. From the Madison Valley near Ennis to the peaks along the west side of the mountains, the elevation rises five thousand feet or more in a matter of a few miles.

Motorized travel into the Madison Range is limited, but an extensive trail system makes access by foot or horseback feasible nearly anywhere a hunter might wish to explore. Over a quarter-million acres are protected by the Lee Metcalf Wilderness, named for an eminent Montana senator whose influence was critical in protecting the state's wildlands from development.

On the east side of the Gallatin River, Montana's portion of the Gallatin Range sprawls north from the boundary of Yellowstone National Park to just south of the bustling downtown and burgeoning subdivisions of Bozeman. Bounded by the Yellowstone River on its eastern foothills, the range represents the northern tip of what is known by biologists and land managers as the Greater Yellowstone Ecosystem.

Like the Madison Range, the Gallatin is fairly buffered from motorized travel. Except for Trail Creek Road on the range's northern end, no roads cross the mountains from east to west, but numerous spur routes from several major highways provide excellent access to many trails. Geographically, the range consists of a major ridge that angles northeast from Yellowstone Park. Several peaks thrust beyond ten thousand feet in elevation, but travel along the highest portions of the Gallatin Range is much easier than in the Madison Range.

Steep slopes rise to high peaks on the west side of the Madison Range. Hunters willing to tackle this tough terrain find lots of elk.

Historically, logging was an important piece of the Gallatin's economy, although fewer timber cuts have occurred in recent times. Nonetheless, many portions of the range are heavily covered with forests of pine, spruce, and fir. Lower, south-facing slopes are often dominated by sagebrush and grass, with north-facing terrain and higher elevations decked by forest up to the barren peaks above the timberline.

Elk Distribution

Elk roam over virtually all of the Gallatin Range with the exception of the highest, most rugged peaks. On the north side, a sizeable herd inhabits the Center Hill, Pine Mountain, and Wineglass Mountain area. These elk are often observed on ridges south of I-90 west of Livingston, where many winter on private land. South and southwest of Bozeman, elk roam the upper reaches of numerous creek bottoms during the summer, descending to lower slopes along the Gallatin Valley to make their living within eyeshot of the ever-sprawling housing developments that gobble winter range at an alarming rate.

To the south, resident elk are scattered throughout the Gallatin Range to the northern boundary of Yellowstone National Park. These animals winter on the west side of Paradise Valley in the foothills and in Tom Miner Basin or drift into the Gallatin River drainage south of Big Sky. In both of these locations, resident elk mingle with hundreds of migrants from Yellowstone National Park. As herd counts conducted by the MDFWP typically occur in late winter, it is difficult to estimate the number of elk that occupy the Gallatin Range outside Yellowstone Park versus those that summer within the park.

In many respects, the elk herd that occupies the Madison Range is a mirror image of the herd that inhabits the Gallatin. During the summer months, animals are found throughout the mountains, with the exception of the barren peaks. Just like those from the Gallatin, they migrate to the surrounding foothills and valleys and winter with migratory animals from Yellowstone Park.

On the north side of the Madison Range, elk are abundant in the Spanish Creek drainage. They also roam the fine habitat to the west along Cherry Creek and its tributaries, to the Red Knob area and the headwaters

Lone Mountain rises over sagebrush and aspen trees in the Gallatin River valley, which provides winter range (and good hunting) for hundreds of elk.

of Bear Trap Creek. Although elk wander freely throughout the Madison Range, the herds on the northern end of the range are somewhat isolated by the imposing ridges and crags of the Spanish Peaks, which divide the mountains along a ragged line that runs from the northwest to the southeast.

South of the Spanish Peaks, Jack Creek runs westward, joining the Madison River just above Ennis Lake. Though it flows through a narrow canyon of sorts before entering the Madison Valley, the upper forks of Jack Creek drain a network of valleys, meadows, and timbered slopes that represent some of the finest elk habitat in the country. A similar situation exists on the east side of the range along the tributaries of the West Fork of the Gallatin River.

From the West Fork of the Gallatin, good numbers of elk are found to the south in the vicinity of three curiously named streams: First, Second, and Third Yellow Mule creeks. Somewhat further south, elk wade the many tributaries of Taylor Creek as they graze the parks in the shadows of Koch Peak and Woodward Mountain. Wapiti are also plentiful in the drainages north of Hebgen Lake, such as Sage Creek, Cabin Creek, and Teepee Creek.

Resident elk of the Gallatin and Madison ranges are joined on their winter range each year by thousands of animals that migrate from Yellowstone Park to winter along the Madison and Gallatin rivers. However, dramatic declines in the northern Yellowstone elk herd—most probably the result of predation by wolves—have greatly reduced the number of elk found on much of the winter range.

The exact mechanisms that trigger migration aren't fully understood, but the colder temperatures and deep snows of late fall and early winter definitely move elk from the park onto their winter range. Although the movement of elk out of the park onto legally huntable public lands sometimes occurs around or before Thanksgiving, drought conditions and warmer temperatures in recent years have nudged the migration later in the year than what was commonly seen a few decades ago.

Where to Hunt

Ambitious hunters can find access points most places in the Gallatin and Madison ranges, although some good hunting areas require a considerable hike or horseback ride to skirt private holdings.

Gallatin Range

Public access to the Gallatin Range is good in most areas for hunters willing to hike or horseback from a road or trailhead. On the north end of the range, Trail Creek Road runs from I-90 exit 316 in a southeasterly direction over the mountains, then drops into Paradise Valley and connects with U.S. Highway 89 south of Livingston. About four miles south of I-90, Trail Creek Road enters the Gallatin National Forest just east of Chestnut Mountain. It then crosses national forest land for a little over two miles before reentering private holdings. A strip of national forest land two miles wide (north to south) by about nine miles long (east to west) lies east of the road, extending to Wineglass Mountain. Hike-in hunting is possible here and on several adjoining sections of state land, but hunters must be careful not to stray onto private land. Look for the best opportunities early in the season before elk are bumped onto private land and on weekdays later on, when animals may drift back onto public land from private. It's also possible to hunt west of Trail Creek Road around Chestnut Mountain or take the Newman Road (FR 245) from Trail Creek Road to access national forest land around Bald Knob.

On the northwest side of the range, a number of access routes to national forest lands are open to the elk hunter. South of Bozeman, Hyalite Canyon Road (FR 62) is one alternative, but since this area is extremely popular with hikers, campers, and other recreationists, you'll likely need to travel a good distance beyond the road or trailheads to encounter elk. To find this road, take Cottonwood Road south from State Highway 85 just west of Bozeman. After about five miles, hang a left (east) on South 19th Street. It's just a mile down this route to Hyalite Canyon Road, which runs south into the Gallatin National Forest.

Approximately two miles south of Gallatin Gateway on U.S. Highway 191, Little Bear Road veers from the highway to the west. After about three miles, the road enters the Gallatin National Forest as FR 980, providing access to a number of spur roads and trails. Search for elk on the ridges and secluded areas away from human activity.

Upon entry into the Gallatin Canyon, Highway 191 parallels the Gallatin River for roughly forty miles before entering Yellowstone National Park north of West Yellowstone. Abundant access points to the Gallatin Range are found on the east side of this highway. Toward the northern end of the canyon, access and hunting opportunities are good from Squaw Creek Road (FR 132). Look for similar options from trails and roads between Squaw Creek and Big Sky at Swan Creek, Moose Creek and Portal Creek.

In the upper Gallatin River valley south of Big Sky, outfitters and day hunters use two major pack trails for elk hunting. Three miles south of Big Sky, look for Porcupine Creek trailhead on the east side of the highway. Trail 34 departs here, with several side trails branching from 34 further along Porcupine Creek. Roughly ten miles south of Porcupine Creek, Buffalo Horn Creek trailhead provides hiking or horseback access via a trail system near the northern boundary of Yellowstone National Park.

Successful hunters on the west side of the Gallatin Range are those willing to work. Early in the fall, during archery season, most elk inhabit higher elevations near the crest of the range, where they find abundant forage and are least disturbed by humans. A heavy snowfall that nudges wapiti from Yellowstone Park can lead to excellent general-season hunting in the Buffalo Horn and Porcupine Creek areas, but this is the exception, not the rule. Even when elk are moving from Yellowstone, hunters who leave the trails to hunt timbered and remote areas find the greatest success.

The eastern side of the Gallatin Range poses more challenge to elk hunters in terms of public access to the national forest. Just over the divide at the headwaters of Buffalo Horn Creek, cross-country hiking or trail access is good at the upper end of Tom Miner Road (FR 63). This road runs to the southwest from Highway 89 about forty miles south of Livingston. In the same vicinity, Rock Creek Road (FR 993) heads due west, with good trail access to the headwaters of Rock Creek.

Roughly eight miles to the north, several trails fan from Big Creek Road (FR 2500) and the Big Creek trail (180), offering travel to several tributaries of Big Creek. It's a tough climb from Big Creek, but look for the best hunting in the basins and bottoms near the headwaters.

Table 12-1 Gallatin Range

	Low	Moderate	High	Very High
Elk Numbers				●
Hunters Per Square Mile		●		
Hunters Per Elk	●			
Trophy Potential		●		
Remote/Roadless Areas		●		

Madison Range

In the Madison Range, public access to national forest lands is adequate overall but becoming increasingly problematic in certain places because of changes of land ownership. Subdivisions and recreational properties now exclude hunters from a number of areas once open to hunting. That said, the ambitious hunter has plenty of access options, even though it takes extra effort in some places.

The southern end of the range in the Gallatin River valley is well traversed with access roads and trails. Just north of Yellowstone Park, west of Highway 191, Sage Creek trail (11) runs for miles and miles along this creek bottom. Hunt the slopes on either side of the trail, or penetrate further into the national forest or the Monument Mountain Unit of the Lee Metcalf Wilderness via one of the spur trails that branch out from Sage Creek. Right next door to the Sage Creek trailhead, Taylor Fork Road (FR 134) winds its way west from Highway 191. This is a popular route with road hunters, but folks who hike from the road or hit one of the numerous trails that fan out from the road find the best hunting.

Roughly ten miles south of Gallatin Gateway on Highway 191, Spanish Creek Road (FR 982) cuts through historic ranchland before winding its way to the Spanish Creek Ranger Station on the South Fork of Spanish Creek. Forest Service trails 401 and 407 depart from the ranger-station area, yielding one of the few public-access points to the northeast portion of the Madison Range. Hunting can be quite good in this area, but many elk often move onto private land in the Spanish Creek drainage early in the general season.

Of the four compass points, access is easiest on the south end of the Madison Range. About five miles west of Highway 191 on U.S. Highway 287, Red Canyon Road (FR 681) gives access to the upper parts of this fairly narrow drainage and terminates at trail 205 that heads north toward the Red Canyon Creek–Teepee Creek divide. Approximately two miles north of the Highway 287 junction on Highway 191, Teepee Creek Road offers numerous access options via several trails and gated roads to the headwaters and high basins on the upper end of Teepee Creek. Early in the general season and during archery season, look for elk in the high country near the drainage divides. At Earthquake Lake, it's well worth a

Table 12-2 Madison Range

	Low	Moderate	High	Very High
Elk Numbers				•
Hunters Per Square Mile		•		
Hunters Per Elk	•			
Trophy Potential		•		
Remote/Roadless Areas			•	

stop at the nearby visitor's center to learn more about the 1959 earthquake that created the lake. Just north of Earthquake Lake, Beaver Creek Road (FR 985) serves as a jumping-off route to many good elk destinations via multiple trails that depart from this road. Hunt north toward the divide of the Madison River–Gallatin River drainages, or explore one of the many tributaries of Beaver Creek.

On the west side, several routes lead to the Gallatin National Forest and the Lee Metcalf Wilderness. Access is possible almost directly west of Ennis in the Jack Creek drainage via Jack Creek Road (FR 166) but may require a one- to six-mile hike on an easement through private land to reach the national forest. South of Ennis on Highway 287, several trails head into the Lee Metcalf Wilderness. East of Cameron, look for Bear Creek Road, which runs about eight miles before reaching the national forest. Several trails are found in this vicinity that generally follow creek drainages into the interior of the mountains. About nine miles south of Cameron, Indian Creek Road winds about six miles east before reaching trail 328 on (you guessed it) Indian Creek. Another fifteen miles down the highway from Indian Creek Road, look for national forest access at Papoose Creek (via trail 355) near Lyon.

Hunting Strategies

There's a healthy elk population in these two aesthetically pleasing mountain ranges, but it's the hunters willing to hike or ride that find them. Just a couple of seasons ago, I hunted the southern end of the Madison Range from a popular trailhead. I hiked about two miles up the trail, then veered off to hunt the timber and tiny parks on a huge forested slope. Just before dark, I shot a big-bodied bull, the seventh brow-tined—and therefore legal—animal I'd seen that day. As I finished retrieving the boned meat and antlers to the parking lot the next day with a sled, a teenage boy on a four-wheeler motored over to appraise my kill.

"I'd like to shoot an elk like that," he confessed wistfully.

I informed him of the numerous wapiti I'd encountered not far up the trail and encouraged him to make the hike. He seemed interested but then enthusiastically told me about the motorized route his dad and he planned to ride that evening. "Maybe I'll find an elk there," he said hopefully. I wished him luck, in a half-hearted sort of way, knowing that unless he got away from his mechanical steed his odds of finding an elk were slim indeed.

Beyond penetrating remote country, hunters in the Gallatin and Madison ranges should keep several other factors in mind. During archery season and even into the general season when the weather is mild, elk often stay at high elevations. If you don't find animals or their fresh sign, turning your boots up the mountains is often the best route to success.

Predators are another factor. Prior to denning, grizzly bears roam over the southern portions of both mountain ranges. Both bowhunters and rifle hunters need to be alert for bear activity in these areas. Wolves are also abundant in these ranges. Many folks believe that wolf predation has made it harder for human hunters to find elk. Although that's not a firmly established conclusion, wolf activity seems to splinter elk herds into smaller groups. Human activity usually chases them into cover. If that doesn't suggest patiently hunting for small bands in the timber, we're not hunting elk in the same world.

Finally, if it's feasible to hunt the later part of the general season, this often yields excellent opportunities in these mountains. Even if it's too warm and the snow cover is too shallow to move migrating elk from Yellowstone Park, resident elk are generally found in higher numbers at lower elevations toward the end of the season. However, oftentimes they hang tantalizingly above their winter range in the valleys until the end of hunting season.

One year, my older brother and I spotted several large groups at daylight on the high ridges above the Madison Valley north of Papoose Creek. With no indication of animals lower down, we hiked up and up and up, finally busting into a major herd that splintered into a dizzying whirl of tan bodies and churning brown legs. Bulls veered in several directions, but I couldn't pick a shot. When the commotion subsided, I walked further up the ridge into several acres of ground that literally looked like an elk barnyard. If you have the ambition to get there, you'll often find numerous elk in staging areas above traditional range when hunting later in the general season.

13

GRAVELLY RANGE, SNOWCREST RANGE, CENTENNIAL MOUNTAINS

-------------◆-------------

Geographical Overview

The mountains of southwest Montana—the Gravelly, Greenhorn, Snowcrest, and Centennial ranges—are thought by many to possess more of an Old West aura than any others in the state. The region is still largely unsettled, except for cattle outfits in the lower river valleys and the occasional guest ranch or small subdivision. Most of the landscape remains as it was a century ago, remote and insulated from the pressures of real estate development and tourism that have so profoundly altered much of the Treasure State. With the exception of the western flank of the Gravelly Range, there's no casual access into these mountains. Penetrating the heart of these ranges involves a thirty- to seventy-mile trek on gravel roads maintained by a county crew whose priorities lie with the taxpayers much closer to the seat of government.

Of these ranges, the Gravelly is the largest and somewhat unique. In contrast to the stern, imposing pinnacles of the Madison Range just across the Madison River, the Gravelly Range is a lower, more gently contoured feature of the landscape. Black Butte, the highest point in the range, rises an impressive 10,545 feet above sea level. However, the towering dark summit is an anomaly, a lone watchman over an undulating plateau of lush creek bottoms, timbered ridges, moist aspen groves, and sprawling slopes thick with grass and aromatic sage. Most of the Gravelly Range consists of fabulous elk habitat from sixty-five hundred feet to eighty-five hundred feet in elevation. It's easy country to hike and hunt. Additionally, the range

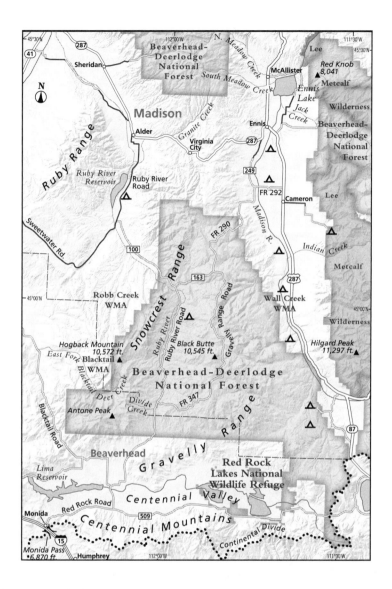

is heavily roaded. Folks who want to pursue wapiti away from droning four-wheelers and pickups find plenty of elk in the Gravellys but also frustration with the lack of solitude.

The Ruby River drains the west side of the Gravelly Range, also drawing its pristine water from creeks that splash from the steeper terrain of the Snowcrest Range, on the western side of the river. Though separated from the Gravellys by the few miles of the Ruby River valley, the Snowcrest Range is notably different from the Gravelly. The mountains are more rugged, with numerous peaks soaring beyond ten thousand feet, flanked by severely canted ridges. Vehicle access is much more limited as well. Several roads provide access for hunting, but none cross the range. Vegetation is similar to that found in the Gravelly Range—heavily timbered north-facing slopes rise to open ridges. Grassy parks and aspen groves sprinkled with evergreens dominate the south-facing slopes, yielding superb habitat for elk and moose. The Snowcrest Range is a stunning setting for an elk hunt but one most suited to hearty souls willing to thin the soles of their boots to find the dark-maned bulls that hide in the evergreen thickets of these mountains.

South of the Snowcrest and Gravelly ranges along the Idaho border, Montana's side of the Centennial Mountains rises above the winsome Centennial Valley. For more than fifty miles, the Continental Divide twists along the spine of the Centennial Range on the Montana-Idaho border east of Monida Pass before veering north along the drainage divide

This is a typical animal for the mountains of southwest Montana in typical terrain. The author downed it at daylight with a modern muzzleloader.

that separates the headwaters of the Red Rock River from those of the Henry's Fork of the Snake River.

Unlike most other mountain ranges in this part of the state, which run roughly north and south, the Centennials wind east and west. Much of the Continental Divide along the crest is in excess of nine thousand feet, with several peaks nearly scratching ten thousand. On Montana's side the range is dominated by steep slopes, broken here and there by flatter benches and basins. Public access is good in the Centennials, with an appealing mix of territory well within the reach of roads but also numerous remote pockets largely buffered from human travel.

Elk Distribution

Elk are plentiful in this entire region. However, their distribution varies markedly with the season. As temperatures rise and bugs become bothersome in the heat of summer, it's common to find bachelor bands of bulls or cows with calves well above timberline, grazing the open ridges and mountaintops, where alpine breezes give some relief from the insects and daytime temperatures remain cool. Here they'll often stay well into the fall, until snow covers the forage and bitterly cold winds send them down from the mountaintops to more sheltered haunts.

How high will they roam? I've seen elk at nearly ten thousand feet on the west side of the Snowcrest Range the evening before the general season opened in late October. Last fall I watched a herd of some thirty animals bed on a wickedly steep slope, in the rocks just above timberline. These elk were completely undisturbed by hunters. I guess the fact that they chose a feeding and bedding area *above* two mountain goats that lolled on a rocky knob in the neighborhood had something to do with it.

Although they summer near the summits of southwestern mountain ranges, elk winter on the dry, open slopes of the foothills or descend to the river valleys. In the Gravelly Range, numerous elk descend to the Wall Creek WMA just south of Indian Creek in the Madison River valley and similar sheltered areas to escape the deep snows at higher elevations. Wapiti from the Snowcrest Range move westward by the hundreds to pass the hard weeks of winter on the Blacktail and Robb Creek-Ledford WMAs, which are located in the foothills and sage flats west and north of the mountains.

Elk from the Snowcrest, Gravelly, and Centennial ranges also winter in the lowlands of the Centennial Valley, where they may be joined by animals from as far away as Yellowstone National Park. In fact, interchange of elk between the Centennial Mountains and the Snowcrest and Gravelly ranges occurs across the Centennial Valley on an ongoing basis.

Where to Hunt

Access to public lands is good over most of this region. Depending on your preferences, you can hunt out the door of a motor home near a well-traveled road or pitch a backpacker's tent miles from the nearest vehicle.

Gravelly Range

The Gravelly Range offers numerous options for motorized access. Gravelly Range Road (FR 290) follows the spine of the range from north to south, with multiple spur roads heading out from this main artery. This route receives heavy traffic during the hunting season, but is ideal for folks wishing to cover lots of ground or quickly scout for an area that's to their liking. From the east side of the range, FR 292 connects to Gravelly Range Road from U.S. Highway 287 south of Ennis near the Varney Bridge fishing-access site. To the west several routes connect to Gravelly Range Road from Ruby River Road. The Ruby River Road runs south from State Highway 287 south of Sheridan at Alder. From Alder this route passes the Ruby River Reservoir, then continues through the Ruby Valley. About five miles south of the Ruby Reservoir, veer left to stay on

Table 13-1 Gravelly Range

	Low	Moderate	High	Very High
Elk Numbers				●
Hunters Per Square Mile			●	
Hunters Per Elk		●		
Trophy Potential	●			
Remote/Roadless Areas		●		

Ruby River Road (don't take Sweetwater Road). Another eight miles up the route, stay left again to avoid Ledford Creek Road. Another six miles or so leads to the first access to Gravelly Range Road. Look for FR 163 a couple of miles beyond the point at which the road pinches near the river at the gap between the ends of the Snowcrest and Greenhorn ranges. Approximately eight miles to the south, FR 1012 at Burnt Creek also connects to Gravelly Range Road. Toward the south end of the Gravelly Range, FR 347 provides access from Ruby River Road at Divide Creek.

Elk hunters seeking a backcountry experience in a nonmotorized area in the Gravelly Range are advised to focus on the southeastern portion of the mountains. Road closures in the Wall Creek and upper Elk River areas provide security for elk and solitude for hunters. Hike-in access to the Elk River region is good from FR 209. Look for this route departing from U.S. Highway 287 about nine miles north of its junction with state Highway 87 near the West Fork camping and picnic areas.

Snowcrest Range

Motorized access is limited in the Snowcrest Range, but fine hunting is to be had by those willing to hike or ride horseback. Ruby River Road

Hunters head into the Snowcrest Range on horseback. Roads are few, but there's a good trail system for riding or hiking.

Table 13-2 Snowcrest Range

	Low	Moderate	High	Very High
Elk Numbers				●
Hunters Per Square Mile			●	
Hunters Per Elk		●		
Trophy Potential	●			
Remote/Roadless Areas		●		

provides numerous points of entry on the east side of the mountains. Hunters who scour the ravines and basins on the upper ends of the creek bottoms find the most elk. Toward the south end of the range, several trails in the Divide Creek area (access it from Ruby River Road) provide entry into the headwaters of Divide, Swamp, and Jones creeks.

On the west side of the Snowcrests, a couple of major points of access are found from Blacktail Deer Creek Road (202 or Blacktail Road), which begins on the south edge of Dillon. It's a long pull, some forty-five miles or so, from Dillon to the western foothills of the Snowcrests. From Blacktail Road, watch for FR 963, which provides access to the southwest portion of the Snowcrest Range via the East Fork of Blacktail Deer Creek. Further along, FR 325 leads to the national forest and a good system of trails, west of Antone Peak. Another option is to take Ledford Creek Road or Robb Creek Road from Ruby River Road south of the Ruby River Reservoir. Both of these gravel routes provide access along the west side of the Snowcrests. For the most part hunting is at its best on the west side of these mountains in late season, when elk begin to move toward their wintering grounds in the western foothills of the range.

Centennial Mountains

Entry into the Centennial Mountains is best found from Red Rock Road, which runs from Monida, just north of the Idaho line on I-15 south of Lima, to the western shore of Henry's Lake, Idaho, just off State Highway 87. This road parallels the north side of the mountain range. A number

Table 13-3 Centennial Mountains

	Low	Moderate	High	Very High
Elk Numbers			•	
Hunters Per Square Mile		•		
Hunters Per Elk		•		
Trophy Potential	•			
Remote/Roadless Areas		•		

of spur routes lead from this main road into the mountains. Generally speaking, the Centennials are steeper toward the west side of the range. On the southern side of Red Rock Lakes National Wildlife Refuge, Centennial Mountains Wilderness Study Area is closed to wheeled vehicles but offers elk hunting via your own two legs or the four of a mountain steed. Hunting in the Centennials has something of a hit-or-miss reputation among Montana natives. There is considerable and unpredictable movement of elk between Montana and Idaho. Migration to and from other areas also affects the number of elk on Montana's side of the Centennials. Additionally, some hunters strongly believe that wolf activity in the area has disrupted historical patterns of habitat use by elk in the Centennials over the last several years. Nonetheless, some older-age bulls are taken from these mountains by persistent hunters.

Hunting Strategies

For both resident and nonresident elk hunters, this region is a highly popular destination for several reasons. First of all, nonproblematic access to vast expanses of public land simplify the "where to go" aspect of the hunt. Second, elk are numerous. Most hunters see enough animals to keep them coming back. Finally, the open character and relatively easy hiking in many portions of these mountains yields a hunt with good probability for success that's not as physically demanding as that found in many other places.

Although this region represents one of the best destinations in the state for novice and do-it-yourself nonresidents to tag an elk, many, many hunters return empty-handed each fall. One of the biggest impediments to success is hunting too close to the roads. A multitude of research studies underscore the fact that elk don't like vehicles or the humans that drive them. To do well in this region, use the roads to get where you want to hunt, then get out and hike—that's the best way to get an elk.

Additionally, pay strict attention to the security needs of your quarry. You might catch elk out in the open at dawn on the first day of the season. However, they get educated in a hurry. Once the rifles start cracking, look for their big tan bodies tucked away in the timber. Sneaking through heavy cover, still-hunting as it's called, is a proven strategy in this neck of the woods. I've killed numerous bulls in the Snowcrest Range; most of them were found in the heart of the timber. Where cover is scattered, get together several members of your hunting party and make a drive. Send a couple of hunters into the evergreens, but place the others along likely escape routes. You might be surprised how many elk are stacked in a small timbered ravine.

Elk are scattered all across these mountains, but they're often concentrated in specific areas. As a general rule, where you find one herd, more are hanging nearby. If you're not finding elk, or recent signs of their presence in the form of fresh tracks and droppings, stay on the move. Once you jump several elk in a specific drainage, stick with it.

The biggest portion of the bull harvest in this region consists of two-and-a-half- and three-and-a-half-year-old bulls with four or five points on each antler that compete aggressively during the rut. This commends the area to bowhunters, who find stags that bugle frequently and often respond quickly to mouth-blown bugles or cow calls. The weather is sometimes very warm during the archery season. When it's comfortable to hunt in your shirtsleeves, look for elk high on the mountains or cooling their hooves in the shade of the timber.

As the elk in these mountains routinely migrate to lower elevations to winter, late-season hunters often find large groups of animals in fairly open country on or adjacent to wintering areas, provided there is enough snow to get them moving. Hitting the hills at dawn to intercept elk as they move between feeding and bedding areas often yields the best success for late-season hunters.

14

TOBACCO ROOT, HIGHLAND MOUNTAINS

------------◆------------

Geographical Overview

Though smaller in size than many mountain ranges in Montana, viewed from the east side, the Tobacco Root Mountains dominates the horizon like the Tetons in Wyoming's famous Jackson Hole. Located south of I-90 between Butte and Bozeman, the heart of the range is a stony ridge with nearly thirty summits exceeding ten thousand feet in elevation. The northwest face of the mountains is exceedingly steep, inhospitable to hunters, and generally poor habitat for elk. The southern end of the range drops from the ridge in an amalgam of open benches, lightly timbered slopes, and basins. Frenzied mining activity in past decades scarred this beautiful range in places, but its effects are fairly isolated.

Most of the Tobacco Roots lies within the Deerlodge National Forest. Isolated parcels of state and BLM land border the national forest in the foothills, increasing public access for individuals handy with a map. The steep character of much of this range, coupled with heavy timber, provides good security for elk.

Just across the Jefferson River valley on the west side of the Tobacco Roots, the Highland Mountains have long been the playground of the rough and tumble mining community of Butte. The Highlands tend to be a heavily timbered range at upper elevations—the spindly lodgepole pines are so thick in places it's impossible to see more than a few rods into the forest. Like the Tobacco Roots, the Highlands have a long history of mining activity, which resulted in the construction of numerous roads. It's easy for hunters to get around on these, but they also contribute to low security for elk and other game animals. The MDFWP estimates that 80 percent of this area represents hunting characterized by "moderate to high levels of motorized access."

Like the Tobacco Roots, most of the Highland Mountains are found within the Deerlodge National Forest. On the southern end of the range, large expanses of BLM land offer additional opportunities for public hunting and recreation.

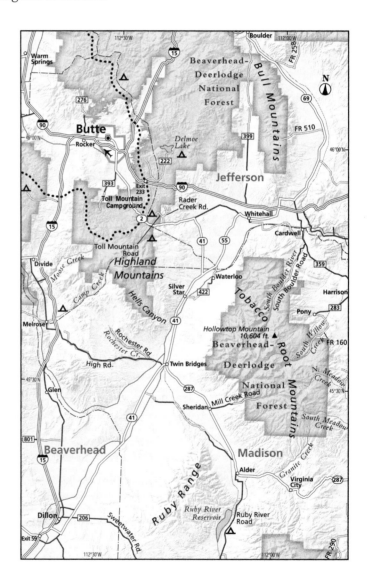

The Tobacco Root Mountains loom above the Jefferson River valley. Under the towering peaks, elk herds roam basins and ridges below timberline.

Elk Distribution

The best habitat, and therefore the greatest numbers of elk in the Tobacco Root Mountains, tends to occur on the east and south portions of the range. Elk typically spend the summers on the ridgetops and meadows at higher elevations, dropping to the foothills during the winter. Wildlife managers estimate that roughly 70 percent of winter range for Tobacco Root elk is found on agricultural lands at lower elevations. On the southwest side of the mountains, elk are scattered from the Mill Creek vicinity, eastward to the headwaters of Granite Creek. On the southeast side, the two forks (north and south) of Meadow Creek drain prime elk habitat where wapiti roam in good numbers. Elk track the upper basins and creek bottoms of the Willow Creek drainages and are also found on the bench that divides North Meadow Creek and South Willow Creek west of Sugarloaf Mountain.

North of the Willow Creek forks, the country tends to become a little steeper. The South Boulder River is the primary stream that drains this area. Elk are found in this drainage, especially along the open ridgetops that separate the tributaries of this small river. Some elk also make their home on the northern end of the Tobacco Roots but spend much of their time on private lands.

Elk distribution in the Highland Mountains is similar to that of many mountainous areas in Montana—small bands of animals are sprinkled throughout suitable habitat from late spring to early winter, concentrating in higher numbers during the lean months of winter in the foothills. As the Highlands aren't a particularly high range and lack the jagged peaks of the Tobacco Roots, elk here are more widely dispersed.

In the summer wapiti frequent lofty elevations among aromatic groves of Douglas fir and lodgepole pine. Years of abundant rainfall produce excellent forage in the uplands where elk herds will remain late into the fall as long as there's plenty to eat. Snow and colder temperatures push them into the foothills.

Where to Hunt

National forest, state, and BLM lands provide a diverse mix of public hunting in the mountains covered in this chapter. Additional opportunities for elk hunting are found on some block management properties.

Tobacco Root Mountains

Public access is reasonably easy in the Tobacco Roots but is generally concentrated in fewer areas than in many other mountain ranges. Near Ennis, North and South Meadow Creek Roads offer easy access to good elk habitat. Look for these routes on the west side of U.S. Highway 287 at McAllister. Roughly one-and-a-half miles from McAllister, North Meadow Creek Road splits from South. Both roads eventually reach the national forest, but over a thousand acres of BLM land are accessible north of the road adjacent to the national forest. If you decide to hunt this BLM area, it's imperative to study property boundaries carefully. On national forest land, hunt pockets on the upper reaches of both North and South Meadow Creek, but don't assume that the end of the road leads to the best hunting. Watch for places that seem unlikely destinations for other hunters—there you'll often sneak into the private haunts of elusive elk.

Some older bulls roam the Tobacco Root Mountains. Thick stands of timber are the best place to find them.

Not far north of North Meadow Creek, the South Willow Creek area near the historic old town of Patosi provides an attractive access point to the Tobacco Roots. South Willow Creek Road (FR 160) can be reached in one of two ways. At Harrison take the narrow highway to Pony (State Highway 283 or Pony Road) west from Highway 287. Watch for South Willow Creek Road, which heads south from Pony. Alternatively, take Norwegian Creek Road less than a mile south of Harrison, west of Highway 287. This road connects with South Willow Creek Road roughly eight miles from the highway. Several trails branch out from South Willow Creek Road once it enters the national forest. Trails 304 and 303 provide good hike-in access to the benches and basins below Patosi Peak. Hunting can also be good southwest of South Willow Creek Road between South Willow Creek and North Meadow Creek. Additionally, the headwaters of North Willow Creek can be gained by taking FR 191 west of Pony. Elk are scattered through the headwaters of North Willow Creek, in the Basin Lakes area, and northward to the upper reaches of Cataract Creek. The soaring summit of Hollowtop Mountain provides an exceptionally scenic backdrop for a hunt.

Table 14-1 Tobacco Root Mountains

	Low	Moderate	High	Very High
Elk Numbers		●		
Hunters Per Square Mile			●	
Hunters Per Elk			●	
Trophy Potential	●			
Remote/Roadless Areas		●		

Moving again northward, good access to the northeast portion of the Tobacco Roots is found along South Boulder Road about five miles south of Cardwell on State Highway 359. This route winds deep within the mountains, to the mostly abandoned but historic mining community of Mammoth and beyond as FR 107. However tempting it may be to chug your way to the end of this road, better hunting is likely to be found north of the route shortly after it enters the national forest. A narrow strip of private land runs intermittently along much of South Boulder Road and is generally well signed. However, it's the hunter's responsibility to stay on public lands, so take care to begin your hunt only on segments that clearly ensure public access.

On the south end of the Tobacco Roots, access is possible from the west side via Mill Creek Road, which runs east from State Highway 287 at Sheridan. National forest lands tend to be steeper on this side of the range, but there are elk to be found in the Mill Creek drainage and to the south along Ramshorn Creek. A bit further south Granite Creek Road (FR 161) leads to the southernmost portion of the Tobacco Roots. Hunt west from this road toward the headwaters of the several tributaries of Granite Creek that drain this area. Toward the latter portion of the general season (mid- to late November), don't overlook the scattered blocks of BLM and state land that abut the national forest.

Highland Mountains

Depending on your style of hunting, your frustration in the Highland Range may stem from too much vehicle access versus too little. With few exceptions, it's a challenge to find seclusion.

In the Butte area, numerous routes lead into the Highlands. State Highway 2 loops over the top of the range south of I-90, crossing the Continental Divide at Pipestone Pass. Several roads branch from this highway.

FR 84 departs Highway 2 about two miles west of Pipestone Pass. This route, also known as Highland Drive, winds through the mountains for about twenty miles before connecting with I-15 at exit 111 on the west side of the range. A number of spur roads depart from this route, yielding additional driving access.

Roughly three miles east of Pipestone Pass, FR 668 provides entry into the Fish Creek area. Hiking is tough in some places, but hunting south of the road near the national forest boundary is attractive, as it is one of the few roadless areas in the Highlands.

On the south side of the Fish Creek–Hell's Canyon divide, Hell's Canyon Road offers another jumping off point into the backcountry. Hell's Canyon Road (FR 125) runs west of State Highway 41 about six miles south of Silver Star. Depending on the conditions, there's good hunting to be found by hiking into the roadless areas north and south of the Hell's Canyon Guard Station. Look for elk around the heads of numerous ravines in the vicinity.

Table 14-2 Highland Mountains

	Low	Moderate	High	Very High
Elk Numbers	●			
Hunters Per Square Mile		●		
Hunters Per Elk				●
Trophy Potential	●			
Remote/Roadless Areas	●			

From the west, Moose Creek Road runs east of I-15 at exit 99 and winds into the central portion of the Highlands. From its junction with I-15, the road crosses some large expanses of BLM land before entering the national forest. Elk are occasionally found in this area, but there are a few scattered parcels of private land along the road, so be aware of your location before departing the road to hunt. Six miles south on I-15, Camp Creek Road also winds through BLM ground before reaching the national forest and provides another point of entry into the western portion of the Highland Range.

Hunting Strategies

Based on research conducted by the MDFWP, elk hunters are generally satisfied with their experience in the Tobacco Root Mountains, but crowding is an often-heard complaint. Most elk hunters tend to be conventional thinkers—trailheads and barricades at the ends of roads are where they park and begin to hunt. In places like the Tobacco Roots, where access routes are limited, this typically concentrates many hunters into a few areas.

To counteract that phenomenon, don't be afraid to set out from a different location. You can't legally or ethically block a road with your vehicle, but if there's room to pull over in a spot away from the trailhead that looks "elky," give it a try. During archery season, look for elk in the dark timber on or near the steep flanks of the central ridge that juts to the peaks of the Tobacco Roots. Stick around late in the evening and hike to your hunting area in the dark before sunrise. That's when you'll hear the bulls bugling and encounter the least interference from other hunters. Although elk harvest in the Tobacco Roots pales in comparison to destinations like the Gravelly Range, there's a fair population of older-age bulls that use the heavy timber and rough terrain to escape hunters. MDFWP harvest statistics indicate that around 20 percent of the bulls taken from the area boast six tines on at least one antler.

Most elk found on national forest land in the Tobacco Roots in the summer and fall pass the winter on private land. In the later part of the general season, hunting is often best on public tracts at lower elevations, adjacent to wintering areas on private land. Access to elk can also be found on some private lands open to public hunting—a number of block management properties are generally found in the foothills of the Tobacco Roots.

Pretty much without exception, elk harvest in the Highlands is highly weather dependent. Early snows nudge animals toward the mid- to low elevation slopes, which are very open and easy to hunt. When that happens, the elk kill spikes considerably. Because of the low habitat security and numerous roads in much of the range, bulls usually run into a bullet at a young age, often before their third birthdays.

If you can swing a few days off before the opening of archery or the general season, it's time well invested in the Highlands. Given the open character of much of the elk habitat, fairly high hunting pressure, and persistent vehicle travel, finding and targeting a particular animal or herd to hunt opening day is an excellent strategy.

The best opportunities for solitude and the greatest chance of encountering a bull larger than a short-beamed four- or five-point are found on the southeast side of the range. Lugging a backpack camp a couple of miles or more from vehicle access is an excellent option for archery hunters. Temperatures are usually mild during the archery season, so a backpack trip is usually comfortable and makes it possible to hunt roadless areas without hiking in and out each day. If you're experienced and have good equipment, a backpack can be just the ticket to fine hunting in the Highlands' backcountry during the early part of the general season as well.

15

BEAVERHEAD, TENDOY, PIONEER, FLEECER MOUNTAINS

------------◆------------

Geographical Overview

If you like the cold, the weather of southwestern Montana just east of the Continental Divide holds great appeal. Wisdom, a hardy hamlet of some 150 residents in the Big Hole Valley, routinely turns up (or should we say down) some of the coldest temperatures in the state—and the entire nation. Twenty degrees below zero on the Fahrenheit scale scarcely raises an eyebrow in this high mountain valley, where temperatures sometimes plunge to minus fifty. Bannack, Montana's first Territorial Capital, lies on the southern end of the Pioneer Mountains along Grasshopper Creek. Temperatures below minus sixty have been recorded in Bannack, perhaps one of the reasons this once-thriving mining community is now a ghost town.

The southernmost mountains of this region, the Tendoy Mountains and the southern portion of the Beaverheads (which span the Montana-Idaho divide), tend to support less timber cover than many other Montana ranges. North-facing slopes are often shaded with thick stands of lodgepole pine and fir, but those with southern exposure commonly sprout sagebrush, grass, and shimmering stands of quaking aspens.

Just south of Clark Canyon Reservoir, the Tendoy Mountains rise to maximum elevations of just over ninety-five hundred feet above sea level. Lower slopes are generally forestless, but mixed stands of conifers thrive at higher elevations. These mountains receive heavy motorized use, making the Tendoys a poor choice for a

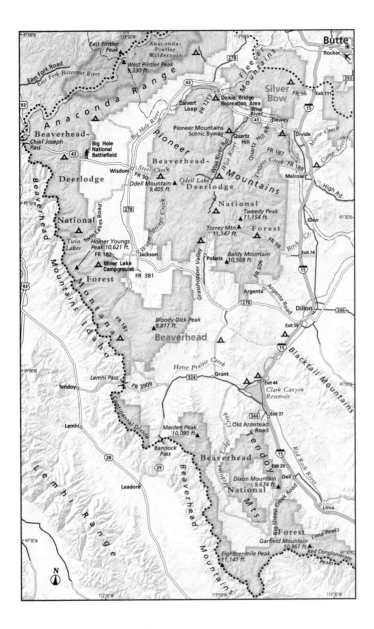

wilderness-type elk hunt. South of the Tendoys, though, the Lima Peaks and Red Conglomerate Peaks along the Idaho border are managed with vehicle restrictions that promote horseback or hike-in hunting in a splendid setting. Montana's portion of the Beaverhead Mountains south of Lemhi Pass is characterized by rather steep ridges rising to treeless summits that regularly exceed ten thousand feet. Public lands are restricted to a narrow strip of the Beaverhead National Forest and BLM acreage (whose width seldom extends more than a few miles) that roughly parallels the Montana-Idaho border.

By contrast the section of the Beaverhead Mountains north of Lemhi Pass is generally more timbered, not as steep (except near the summits) and boasts larger expanses of public land that often cover a breadth of ten or more miles from the mountaintops to the Big Hole Valley.

The Pioneer and Fleecer mountains sprawl across the northern portion of this region, separated only by a narrow valley on the upper end of the Big Hole River. Both ranges are quite heavily timbered in lodgepole pine and other conifers. The Wise River flows from south to north through the Pioneers, separating them into two distinct sections often described as the East Pioneers and West Pioneers. In general, the eastern section is more rugged country that rises to significantly higher elevations

Open country, aspens, and evergreens dominate remote areas in the Lima Peaks vicinity, creating beautiful scenery and excellent elk hunting.

than the west. Several peaks top eleven thousand feet in the East Pioneers, but few scratch above nine thousand feet to the west. Overall, the Pioneer Mountains are remote and possess several large, roadless sections. This factor, coupled with their heavy cover, allows a fairly high percentage of bull elk to reach maturity even though there are no formally designated wilderness areas in the range or restrictive hunting regulations.

Elk Distribution

Elk utilize the Tendoy Range similarly to the manner in which they occupy many mountainous areas of the state. Summer finds them grazing the highest ridges and basins while winter snow pushes them to the foothills and valleys. On the west side of the Tendoys, elk winter on the lowlands along Medicine Lodge Creek. They also favor the foothills on the eastern side in the Red Rock River valley. From these major wintering areas, they disperse throughout the mountains during the summer. However, during dry years wapiti often drop from the southeast side of the Tendoys to raid alfalfa fields and other croplands along the Red Rock River.

Further south, elk from the Lima Peaks and Red Conglomerate Peaks areas winter north of their summer range in the Little Sheep Creek area and the foothills south of Lima. From here they migrate up the creek bottoms in the spring, ranging high along the Continental Divide in the heat of the summer, where some interchange of elk occurs between the Montana and Idaho sides of the divide.

The sinuous path of the Beaverhead Mountains winds over a hundred miles through this region. Montana's western side of the range tends to cover less area than Idaho's acreage on the east. Nonetheless, elk numbers tend to be quite high in the Beaverheads. To the south, animals winter in the valley between the Beaverhead and Tendoy mountains on the upper reaches of the Medicine Lodge and Big Sheep Creek drainages. Toward Bannack Pass and Lemhi Pass, wapiti pass the snowy season in the Bachelor Mountain area southwest of Bannack and the foothills along Horse Prairie Creek, with a sizeable herd also occupying the Trail Creek drainage. Like their southern counterparts, these animals traipse back toward the high country on the Continental Divide during the summer.

North of Lemhi Pass to the end of the Beaverhead Mountains around Chief Joseph Pass on State Highway 43, most elk from the Beaverheads cross the Continental Divide to winter in Idaho. In recent years the MDFWP estimates that up to a thousand head of elk make this interstate trek in the fall, often before the end of Montana's general elk season.

Ringed on three sides by the Big Hole River, the health of the Pioneer Mountains' elk herd remains intimately tied to the valleys carved by the river. Originating southwest of the Pioneers, the Big Hole River flows north, then turns east and finally south, all the while within eyeshot of the mountains. Trace your finger along the foothills between the Pioneer Mountains and the Big Hole River on a map, and you've pretty well identified the winter range of area elk, except for those animals that drift into the Grasshopper Valley and the Rattlesnake Creek drainage to the south.

Given their long legs, large body mass, and ability to subsist on browse and woody plants that aren't normally covered by snow, elk are much more winter hardy than deer or antelope. However, the bitterly cold temperatures and deep snow of the Big Hole River country take a higher toll on Pioneer Mountain elk during tough winters than wapiti feel in most parts of the state. For example, the 1996–1997 winter was hard on elk over most of Montana but especially difficult in the Big Hole, where winterkill and a poor calf crop the following spring caused a significant drop in numbers. Elk in the East Pioneers tend to fare better in the winter than those in the western portion of the mountains—overall numbers tend to be somewhat higher in the east as a result.

Once safely through the winter, elk travel up major creek drainages and disperse throughout the Pioneer Mountains. On the east side, however, dry years sometimes bring animals from the mountains to the Big Hole river bottoms south of Melrose, where they raid hayfields by night and retreat to the foothills to bed by day.

South of Anaconda, elk habitat and population patterns in the Fleecer Mountains are nearly identical to those found in the Pioneers. Animals ascend to higher elevations in the summer after weathering the cold season in the foothills and valleys. Primary wintering areas occur on the northwestern side of the Fleecers on the Mount Haggin WMA and two units of the Fleecer Mountain WMA found northeast and southeast of the mountains. Wintering elk are commonly seen in high numbers west of I-15 southwest of Butte and north of Highway 43 around Divide.

Where to Hunt

The myriad of mountain ranges and public-land destinations draw relatively high numbers of hunters to portions of this region. Additionally, good elk-hunting opportunities are available on block management properties.

Tendoy Mountains

Access to the Tendoy Mountains via motorized vehicles occurs at a handful of points around the range. Once on public land, though, vehicles have the run of the Tendoys—you'll look long and hard for a location that's more than a mile from a vehicle trail, legal or otherwise. A narrow, north-south-lying strip of territory on the eastern side of the range from Dixon Mountain to Timber Butte and then north along the Medicine Lodge Creek–Red Rock River divide holds some of the most remote and highest country in the Tendoys. Look for elk to hole up in the timbered, north-facing slopes in this area until they're pushed lower by wintry weather. Hiking or horseback access to this area is possible from several directions from exit 29 on I-15 about four miles north of Dell. West of this exit watch for several Forest Service routes (957, 964, 959 and 960) that originate in this area. FR 960 heads south, then climbs over a high ridge to drop into the Muddy Creek drainage. Hike-in hunting to the north toward Timber Butte or south toward Dixon Mountain is possible from this route. FRs 959 and 957 wind up in steep, canyon-laced country that also offers hike-in hunting in a fairly remote setting.

Vehicle access to pretty much any other section of the Tendoys can be gained from the road along Muddy Creek on the south end (RD 323) of the range that forks from Big Sheep Creek Road (Big Sheep Creek Backcountry Byway, RD 302). The quickest route to Muddy Creek is via I-15. Exit the interstate at Dell (exit 23) to the frontage road on the west side of the highway. About one mile south, Big Sheep Creek Road heads southwest up its namesake stream. A drive of roughly seven miles leads to Muddy Creek and RD 323 (FR 956). Many branches fan from this trunk,

Table 15-1 Tendoy Mountains

	Low	Moderate	High	Very High
Elk Numbers				•
Hunters Per Square Mile			•	
Hunters Per Elk		•		
Trophy Potential	•			
Remote/Roadless Areas	•			

providing vehicle access just about anywhere you'd like to go on public land, but please stay on established routes!

Toward the end of the general season, elk often move from the high country to lower-lying foothills. Access to many foothills destinations on the west side of the Tendoys is possible from Big Sheep Creek Backcountry Byway where it sporadically crosses BLM lands. Decent numbers of elk are found in the Tendoys, but with fairly heavy hunting pressure and pervasive road access, this isn't the place to look for a trophy bull—the majority of antlered elk taken are young animals with four or five points per antler.

Lima Peaks, Red Conglomerate Peaks

A very different experience awaits hunters in the Lima Peaks and Red Conglomerate Peaks territory south of Lima, an eastern extension of the Beaverhead Mountains. Much of this portion of the Beaverhead National Forest is managed with vehicle restrictions, giving the nod to hunters motivated by solitude versus those who prefer easy access. Two vehicle routes provide entry to the east and west sides of this area, with walk-in hunting available via established trails or cross-country hiking. To the west, Little Sheep Creek Road (FR 3929) departs from near Lima. Take exit 15 from I-15 at Lima, then hit the frontage road on the west side of the highway. About one mile north, watch for Little Sheep Creek Road. This route runs southwest about six miles before entering the national forest, as it follows the Middle Fork of Little Sheep Creek to a trailhead.

Trail 40 heads east toward the Lima and Red Conglomerate Peaks along Little Sheep Creek. Hunt the ridges and timbered pockets to the north and south of the trail.

From the east, access is found via FR 1079. To find this road, leave I-15 at exit 9. Look for FR 1079 on the west side of the highway near Big Beaver Creek. Follow this route about nine miles to the national forest boundary. At this point the road splits. FR 1079 continues about one mile south to a trailhead on Shineberger Creek, which offers trail access to the south and west. The other road, FR 1080, winds west about two miles, then forks at FR 1013. A two-mile drive southwest on FR 1013 leads to a trailhead on Sawmill Creek, at which several trails fan toward the Red Conglomerate Peaks to the south and the Lima Peaks to the north. Again, target the timbered, north-facing slopes and forested basins for the best hunting.

Beaverhead Mountains

Montana's portion of the Beaverhead Mountains that lie west of the Lima Peaks offers a mix of elk hunting from heavily roaded areas to wilderness settings. From Big Sheep Creek Road on the south end of the Tendoy Mountains, Nicholia Creek Road (FR 657) heads south toward a section of wild country in the southernmost region of the state. About ten miles south of Big Sheep Road, FR 657 dead-ends at a trailhead. Trail 91 parallels Nicholia Creek, then loops under the Montana-Idaho divide, offering good hiking or horseback travel in this remote area. This is an ideal place to hunt the edges of timber at dawn and dusk for moving elk—and an inviting spot to kick back and enjoy the quietude.

In the Horse Prairie Creek drainage, options for elk hunting with nearby vehicle access abound. From I-15 south of Dillon, head west from exit 44 onto State Highway 324. About twenty-one miles from the interstate, Lemhi Pass Road (FR 3909) veers to the right up Trail Creek. Near the top of the pass, spur roads fan north and south onto public land. Lots of elk inhabit the Trail Creek drainage, but most get pushed onto private land very early in the hunting season. Cruise the edges between public and private land, and you may catch stray animals away from "elk sanctuaries" created by private landowners in the area who don't allow hunting.

Another option is to swing north on FR 181 that follows Bloody Dick Creek to Reservoir Lake and Bloody Dick Campground. Numerous vehicle trails branch from this road, yielding plenty of places to hunt.

Just before Highway 324 crests Bannack Pass into Idaho, watch for public access roads to the west, providing hunting opportunities on national forest, state, and BLM lands. Hunt high toward the crest of the Continental Divide early in the general season or during archery season, but drop to lower elevations later in the year.

From the headwaters of the Big Hole River to Highway 43's crossing of Chief Joseph Pass, numerous access points are available to national forest lands in the Beaverhead Mountains. Remember, though, that this stretch of country holds a great number of elk that migrate into Idaho, sometimes quite early in Montana's general season. Bowhunting may provide the best opportunity for downing a nice bull in this area, as elk are generally more concentrated on the Montana side of the divide early in the fall, and there's enough cover for bulls to escape all but the most devoted hunters.

From State Highway 278 about eighteen miles south of Wisdom, two routes lead west to the national forest. Skinner Meadows Road (FR 381) heads south toward the headwaters of the Big Hole River and Van Houten Lakes. Spur roads and trails branch from this route, yielding multiple points from which to commence a hunt. Just north of Skinner Meadows Road on Highway 278, FR 182 heads to the Miner Creek drainage and Miner Lake Campground. Again, branch roads and trails provide numerous hunting options.

Table 15-2 Beaverhead Mountains

	Low	Moderate	High	Very High
Elk Numbers			●	
Hunters Per Square Mile			●	
Hunters Per Elk		●		
Trophy Potential	●			
Remote/Roadless Areas		●		

Further north, similar access situations exist in the Twin Lakes and Ruby Creek areas. About four miles south of Wisdom, Twin Lakes Road (FR 945/183) launches west from Highway 278. This route jogs approximately twenty-two miles in a south-west-south-west pattern before reaching Twin Lakes Campground, just a few miles shy of the Montana-Idaho divide. To reach the Ruby Creek area, take Highway 43 about five miles west of Wisdom to Gibbonsville Road (FR 624) found on the south side of the highway. It's about ten miles to the national forest boundary. About two miles beyond the NF boundary, a spur road (FR 943) winds back along the north side of Ruby Creek, offering access to a fairly substantial tract of remote elk habitat to the north.

Pioneer Mountains Overview

Across the Big Hole Valley from the Beaverhead Mountains, options abound for access to public lands in the Pioneer Mountains. On the periphery of the range, more than a dozen entry points provide vehicle access, with many more available to hunters on foot or horseback. Additionally, Wise River Road (FR 73, Pioneer Mountains Scenic Byway) cuts between the East and West Pioneers in the Beaverhead National Forest, offering further access via a number of branch roads and trailheads. Some eight established campgrounds are found along the length of the byway, giving some indication of the popularity of this route with recreationists.

Overall, the Pioneer Mountains offer an appealing mix of backcountry areas and easy motorized access. In addition to traveling established roads in a pickup, some trails are open to access via ATV and/or motorbike. Backcountry hikers and motorized hunters need to carefully check current travel restrictions in the area they plan to hunt to avoid conflicts with other users. This is especially true for ATV and motorbike operators, as illegal activity (riding on closed trails, traveling cross-country) may ultimately lead to increased restrictions.

As an overview, distinct regions of the Pioneers promote different types of hunting. For easy motorized access via pickup or other full-size vehicle, look to the north and south portions of the East Pioneers, the north part of the West Pioneers and branch roads along the Wise River. Semi-backcountry hunting via ATV or motorbike trail is most abundant

The author found this bull in a tiny clearing surrounded by forest at dusk. Similar spots are ideal places to hunt in the Pioneer Mountains.

in the central area of the East Pioneers, with trails launching from the Wise River vicinity or public-access points on the east side of the mountains. A similar area in the West Pioneers is found in the north-central portion of the range between Odell Lake and Round Top Mountain. Nonmotorized, backcountry hunting in a wilderness setting dominates the southern region of the West Pioneers in the upper Wyman and Odell Creek area and the Warm Springs Creek drainage. In the East Pioneers a sizeable chunk of roadless habitat is found along the divide between the Wise and Big Hole rivers from the Baldy Mountain/Estler Lake vicinity north to the Mount Alverson/Tendoy Lake area.

West Pioneers

On the north side of the West Pioneers, FR 1213 launches north from the west side of Highway 43 at Dickie Bridge, then bends to follow Bryant Creek into the mountains. This route provides some ten miles of road access, with a couple of branch roads for yet more driving. However, a number of trails that are closed to vehicles after October 15 also depart from this route. These are definitely of interest to elk hunters looking for a hike-in destination close to a main highway.

On the west side of the West Pioneers, access to the national forest is possible at Doolittle and Steel creeks. To reach the Doolittle Creek area, take Highway 43 about ten miles north of Wisdom, then head east on FR 2421 up Doolittle Creek. Several vehicle trails sprout from this route, some of which have seasonal closures during the general elk season. Hunting along the national forest boundary can be good in this area when elk begin to move from the high country toward the Big Hole Valley. Similar access and hunting opportunities are found to the south in the Steel Creek drainage. Just one mile north of Wisdom, FR 90 runs east of Highway 43 for about five miles before reaching the NF boundary. For backcountry hunting, take FR 2433 south of FR 90 to trail 198, which heads south along the West Fork of Warm Springs Creek.

Of particular note to backcountry hunters is FR 928 on the south side of the West Pioneers. This road springs from Highway 278 about ten miles east of Jackson. The route enters the Beaverhead National Forest less than a mile north of the highway, then continues about six miles before reaching a {T} in the road. FR 220 swings to the west, looping a bit south, then north to the Clemon Cow Camp on Warm Springs Creek, a drive of about nine miles. Several trails spring from the Cow Camp area (167, 401) or from FR 220 (trail 5 at Hunter Creek), yielding access to a large, wilderness-type area to the north. The heart of this region lies deep in the mountains. Expect the best hunting during the archery season and the early days of the general season before elk begin moving toward their winter range in the valleys.

From Wise River Road (FR 73), entry points to the West Pioneers abound. About nine miles south of Wise River (the town), trail 245 runs up Pettengill Creek from FR 185. Several branch trails fan from 245. Currently most of this trail system is open to ATVs and motorbikes, making it very popular with motorized hunters. Those who park their machines and put some miles on their boot soles stand by far the best chance of finding an elk.

Another attractive area for motorized users is found about eight miles south of Pettengill Creek at Lacy Creek. FR 1299 winds four miles west along Lacy Creek from the Wise River Road, leading to several trailheads. Motorized use is possible during hunting season on trails that head north and west, but make sure you clearly understand trail regulations before you head out. To the south, trail 141, which heads up Skull Creek, is restricted to hiking and horseback travel.

Less than two miles south of Lacy Creek, another popular route into the West Pioneer springs from Wise River Road at Wyman Creek. FR 2417 runs about four miles west along the creek, leading to trails that parallel Odell Creek (trail 758) and Wyman Creek (trail 167). These nonmotorized routes lead to the remote interior of the mountains, yielding excellent backcountry destinations for hardy hunters, especially during archery season and the early days of the general season.

East Pioneers

Access to the East Pioneers is also possible from Wise River Road, though more routes open to full-size vehicles are found on the east side of the range. Just north of Lacy Creek, trail 42 is currently open to motorized travel and loops into the headwaters of Little Joe Creek. About one mile north, FR 3976 runs east of Wise River Road for less than a mile to a trailhead that marks the beginning of trails 140 and 152. Trail 140 essentially parallels the Wise River, winding north for several miles. Hunt to the east up the ridges and ravines above the trail. Trail 152 launches up Gold Springs Creek. This is a worthwhile trek that boasts entry into a tract of country south of Maurice Mountain that's closed to motorized travel.

A good-looking bull bedded down in southwestern Montana. Always be prepared to hunt in the snow in elk country.
© Jack Ballard

Rifle season calls for an adequate firearm. The great gun writer Jack O'Connor swore by the .270 but others prefer a .30/06 or .338. Here the author is using a .444 Marlin for hunting in a timbered drainage. © Jack Ballard

Where possible, hunting on horseback covers a lot of ground while scouting, and a pack horse lets the hunter bring out the meat and antlers in one trip. © Jack Ballard

The rut over, a group of big bulls that weeks earlier would have sparred angrily now stands together peaceably at dawn. © Jack Ballard

A bull bugles as the rut gets into full swing. Calling in a bugling bull is one of the most intense challenges a hunter can face, especially while bowhunting. © Jack Ballard

A dominant bull will tend a small herd of cows during the rut, running off lesser bulls that challenge him. Staking out cows, and the areas where they travel, can be an effective tactic. © Jack Ballard

If you end up spending twice the money on binoculars as you spent on your rifle, you did the right thing. Having really good glass and knowing how to use it effectively for hours can make the difference between eating elk steak and another night of beans and franks. © Jack Ballard

By its antlers and body mass, this bull appears to be five years old or more. Field judging racks isn't easy, but focus on the overall mass, length of the tines, and outside spread. © Jack Ballard

Here's a bull with more body mass, but the bull in the previous photo sports a finer rack in terms of tine length. However, either animal is an exceptional trophy. © Jack Ballard

If you can stalk quietly—an easier task in sound-muffling snow—you can get close enough to an elk for a shot with open sights. But most times, elk hunters prefer a gun with a good 3x scope or higher. © JACK BALLARD

A heavy-bodied bull already on the prowl at dawn, bugling in a snowy meadow in southern Montana. As in the previous photo, the smart hunter will have a good snow-and-cold outfit—layers that hold in core heat and keep the extremities functional. © JACK BALLARD

A successful day in the Montana wilderness: A hunter and guide return to camp with a quartered elk and a nice rack atop the pack mule. © Jack Ballard

A wall-tent camp in October. Such canvas tents work well in all kinds of weather and provide a sturdy home for weeks on end. © Jack Ballard

A terrifically handsome trophy bull—thick beams, long tines, and a nice spread. This is the type of Montana bull everyone hopes to kill. But don't get so hung up on antlers that you minimize the accomplishment of any successful elk hunt. © JACK BALLARD

Roughly five miles south of Lacy Creek, a notable trailhead is found adjacent to the Mono Creek Campground. Trail 2 departs east along Jacobsen Creek, climbing to the summit of the East Pioneers near Tahepia Lake. Lower portions of this trail are currently open to motorbikes during hunting season. For backcountry foot and horseback travelers in the general season, trail 56 branches from trail 2 about two miles above the trailhead, veering south along David Creek. This path offers access to a considerable nonmotorized area along the crest of the East Pioneers.

Elsewhere, abundant motorized access awaits on the south side of the East Pioneers. From the south, take Highway 278 west from exit 59 on I-15 south of Dillon. About seven miles west of the interstate, watch for Argenta Road (FR 192) on the north side of Highway 278. A drive of roughly seven miles leads to the Beaverhead National Forest. Two miles beyond, FR 606 (French Creek Road) heads north, with numerous spur roads branching from this main route. FR 606 wanders about fifteen miles north before connecting with Birch Creek Road (FR 98). Although it may be tempting to road hunt this route, folks that strike out even a mile from their vehicle have a much better chance of encountering elk.

Birch Creek Road also runs into the southern portion of the East Pioneers, with easy access from I-15. At exit 74, head west on FR 98 about five miles to the national forest boundary. The route continues west another thirteen miles or so, winding deep into the mountains. Some four miles beyond the NF boundary, FR 8200 shoots north of FR 98 on a twelve-mile course through the evergreens, offering access to high, remote areas near the backbone of the East Pioneers via cross-country hiking or established trails.

Toward the north end of the East Pioneers, the Trapper Creek area provides several venues for vehicle access. From I-15 take exit 93 at Melrose, then head west on Trapper Creek Road (FR 188) approximately eight miles to the Beaverhead National Forest. From here the route runs along the creek, reaching several old mining claims about seven miles in. Hunt on foot to the south, or try one of the spur roads. Alternatively, take FR 187 north of Trapper Creek Road about one-and-a-half miles before the NF boundary. This road leads to a network of branch roads and trails worth exploring in the latter weeks of the general season.

Table 15-3 Pioneer Mountains

	Low	Moderate	High	Very High
Elk Numbers		●		
Hunters Per Square Mile			●	
Hunters Per Elk				●
Trophy Potential^		●		
Remote/Roadless Areas		●		

^ Low in areas with motorized access.

Motorized access to the northernmost section of the East Pioneers abounds via Quartz Hill Road (FR 187). Look for this route about five miles east of Wise River (the town) on the south side of Highway 43. This road whisks through a couple of miles of BLM land before entering the Beaverhead National Forest. A spiderweb of roads fans from this route in the Quartz Hill area, making it possible to cover a lot of ground from the seat of a pickup. But as always, those who spend the most time warming the cab spend the least time butchering elk.

Fleecer Mountains

Numerous access roads snake into the Fleecer Mountains, to the extent that the vast majority of the area is described by the MDFWP as containing "moderate to high levels of motorized access." Nonetheless, the Fleecers harbor plenty of elk. Though this mountain complex is much smaller than the Pioneer Mountains to the south, the Fleecers don't lag much behind the Pioneers in total numbers of wapiti.

On the west side, State Highway 278 (Big Hole/Mill Creek Road) runs through the state-owned Mount Haggin Wildlife Management Area, offering several points of access to the west slope of the Fleecers. About seven miles north of the Highway 278/Highway 43 junction, FR 1000 winds along Moose Creek, terminating a bit west of Bear Mountain. To the east, in the Bear Mountain and Dickie Peak vicinity, lies a good-size chunk of high, remote habitat. Access to this area is also possible

Table 15-4 Fleecer Mountains

	Low	Moderate	High	Very High
Elk Numbers				●
Hunters Per Square Mile				●
Hunters Per Elk		●		
Trophy Potential	●			
Remote/Roadless Areas	●			

from the south. Take FR 1208 about nine miles west of Wise River on the north side of Highway 43. This route heads east along the Big Hole River for about four miles, then turns north and climbs steadily into the mountains. Trail 275 departs from the end of this route, yielding good hiking near Dickie Peak. Expect the best hunting in this area prior to wintry weather, which pushes elk to lower elevations.

Another south-side access road runs along Jerry Creek. FR 83 departs Highway 43 about one-and-a-half miles east of Wise River. The road reaches the national forest just a couple of miles from the highway, with additional access available from spur routes.

From the east, two major routes facilitate access to public hunting. From I-15 at exit 111, Divide Creek Road (FR 96) winds into the mountains, with many branch roads that provide additional driving. Further north, at exit 119 on I-15, head west toward FR 8490, which enters the Deerlodge National Forest in the German Gulch area. South of this route, there's a notable swath of roadless country that rises to the Continental Divide, well worth a scout in your hiking boots.

In addition to state, BLM, and national forest land, don't overlook public hunting opportunities on block management properties in the Fleecer foothills.

Hunting Strategies

Elk habitat in this region runs the gamut from open, sagebrush hillsides, to windswept pastures above timberline, to prickly lodgepole jungles and everything in between. Throw in some logged-over areas and burns, and you've pretty well covered all types of mountainous elk habitat.

In steep, lightly forested areas like those found in the Tendoy Mountains, Lima Peaks, and southern Beaverhead Mountains, it's essential to target animals in their hiding cover. The greater the hunting pressure, the more elk move into nasty, timbered strongholds to elude humans. Look for them especially on north-facing slopes that promote heavier timber growth versus those that receive southern exposure.

Another important aspect of hunting this habitat is elevation. Ridges rise to ten thousand feet in the Lima Peaks. The Montana-Idaho divide routinely slithers over country exceeding nine thousand feet. Elk use these haunts above the timberline to escape September heat and graze on cured alpine grass. Bowhunters often find bugling bulls in the timber just below the tree line, but elk sometimes remain at similar elevations well into the general season, occasionally banding into herds of up to a hundred animals that may contain a dozen or more bulls. Look for these herds at dawn and dusk. If you spot them feeding a particular mountainside just before dark, hunt there early the next morning or evening. In areas of low hunting pressure, elk may drift out of the timber an hour before dark, leaving you sufficient time to make a stalk.

Heavy timber is found over much of the Pioneer Mountains, yielding lots of escape cover for elk. However, the dense stands of evergreens that make ideal spots to bed and hide don't offer wapiti much to eat. As a rule of thumb, I advise novice elk hunters to target timber and other cover in open habitats but do just the opposite in timbered areas. Old clear-cuts, natural meadows, and expanses of burned timber facilitate the production of grasses and shrubs that elk prefer for food.

While your odds of catching elk in the middle of a clearing during hunting season are poor, you will consistently find them on the edges. In the interior of the Pioneers, hunt the timber adjacent to feeding areas. Even if you don't see elk grazing on an old burn, fresh tracks and droppings are sure indications you're in a productive area. Roads with permanent or seasonal vehicle closures are still open to nonmotorized travel. Use them. These routes provide quick access to secure habitat and make retrieving an animal much easier once you've filled your tag.

Given the sprawling character of the Pioneers and the moderate elk numbers, it's essential to be patient. In any situation, taking several years to become familiar with an area is one of the best ways to increase your success as an elk hunter. This is especially true in the Pioneers. Wapiti favor certain drainages over others, sometimes for reasons inexplicable to the human mind. Drought, temperature, and snow depth also affect their movements. The better you understand these factors, the more consistently you'll kill elk.

The harsh winters that sometimes descend on the Pioneer and Fleecer mountains often move animals toward their winter range in the foothills and valleys before the end of the general elk season. After a major storm or anytime in late November, it's advisable to scour lower elevations before pushing far into the mountains. Elk will shy away from areas near the roads, but often a cross-country hike of just a mile or so will put you into the herds. Buy a good map and use it when you hunt the lowlands, as elk may be holed up on the edges between public and private land.

16

BOULDER MOUNTAINS, BULL MOUNTAIN

------------◆------------

Geographical Overview

This area encompasses those mountainous areas north of I-90 from Cardwell to Butte and south of the Blackfoot River from Lincoln to Rogers Pass. These mountains, which flank the Continental Divide from Butte to Rogers Pass, are often described as the Boulder Mountains, although many maps don't make this an official designation. Likewise, the separate range immediately north of I-90 between Whitehall and Cardwell is known locally as Bull Mountain, although that name doesn't appear on all maps.

In general, these mountains range from five thousand to eight thousand feet in elevation, although some isolated peaks are near the nine-thousand-foot level. Several highways span the Continental Divide from east to west in the Boulder Mountains, crossing the nation's backbone at mountain passes that tend to sport elevations of around sixty-three hundred feet. At most elevations the montane portion of this region is quite heavily forested, with fire activity, logging, and some natural clearings providing better forage for elk and other wildlife than the dog-hair stands of lodgepole pine that dominate many places.

Logging and mining activities have created numerous roads and trails in the Boulder Mountains. Many of these are open to vehicle travel all year, making sections of national forest and BLM lands very popular with ATV riders and snow-mobilers, to the point that noticeable displacement of elk occurs in some of the

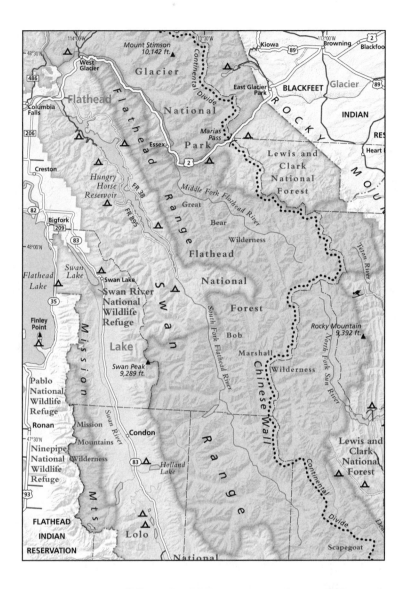

heavily traveled areas. (The MDFWP estimates that in HDs 215, 318, and 335, the vast majority of elk habitat occurs less than a mile from lands open to motorized travel.) Mining claims also dot the mountains, creating small islands of private land surrounded by public. It's essential to know where you're traveling to avoid trespassing.

Human encroachment into winter range is a growing problem in this region, resulting from ever-expanding subdivisions in the Helena area, real estate development in the Blackfoot Valley, and disturbance of

The Boulder Mountains south of Helena are generally low in elevation, but boast high numbers of elk.

big-game animals on public winter range by snowmobiles. Nonetheless, the area supports a healthy population of elk with countless avenues for access to public-land hunting. However, it's also a good place to consider the impacts of your travel on wildlife and a great place to pitch in on conservation efforts by the Rocky Mountain Elk Foundation and other groups working to protect winter range.

Elk Distribution

Elk numbers fluctuate dramatically in many mountain ranges in the state, with gains or losses from one year to the next sometimes representing over 25 percent of the total population. Such is not the case in the Bull Mountain area north of Whitehall. Habitat, hunting pressure, and wintering conditions tend to be fairly consistent, yielding a stable herd of around three hundred animals. Summer finds them spread across the mountains, with many favoring the east side, where the topography isn't quite as steep as the west and where alfalfa fields in the north Boulder River valley provide succulent forage that the animals are happy to raid in dry years.

Similar numbers of elk roam the portion of the Boulder Mountains that lies north of I-90 and south of I-15 from Butte to Boulder. Elk habitat is good on the eastern flank of these mountains, although extensive travel by ATVs on BLM and national forest lands north of Pipestone Hot Springs encourages elk to hole up in steep, isolated areas inaccessible to motorized vehicles. As water sources can be somewhat limited in dry years, elk are normally associated with creek bottoms and adjacent areas, especially those that provide a buffer from ongoing encroachment by humans and vehicles.

North of I-15, west of I-90 and south of U.S. Highway 12, elk are scattered throughout the Boulder Mountains in the summer and fall, moving toward traditional wintering grounds as wintry conditions descend on the high country. East of Deer Lodge, good numbers of elk winter in the foothills in the Fred Burr Creek drainage and adjacent drainages to the north. Summer finds these animals to the southeast in the Electric Peak and Cliff Mountain area or dispersed elsewhere along the west side of the Continental Divide. Elk also winter along the Little Blackfoot River in the vicinity of Elliston and Avon, moving up the Little Blackfoot River and other creek bottoms south of Highway 12 to summer at higher elevations.

On the east side of the Continental Divide, wapiti track the lowlands along the upper portion of the Boulder River west of Basin in the winter. From there they disperse north and south to high basins and ridges east of the divide. Elk are also scattered north, south, and west of Helena, where they must increasingly dodge housing developments.

North of Highway 12 to the Blackfoot River, elk utilize public lands (national forest, state, and BLM) throughout the summer and into the fall. However, most of the winter range (70–80 percent) occurs on private land. Animals are generally accessible to hunters on public land throughout the archery and general seasons, unless nasty weather moves them onto winter range.

To the west, elk dodge the heavy snow at higher elevations in the Nevada Creek valley along State Highway 141 in the Nevada Lake and Helmville area. From here they drift north and east to summer along the Nevada Creek–Blackfoot River divide and the Continental Divide. Elk also move into this area from the north when they depart their wintering grounds along State Highway 200 and the Blackfoot River in the Lincoln area.

East of the Continental Divide, wapiti weather cold months and snow in the Canyon Creek and Little Prickly Pear Creek vicinity east of Granite Butte. These animals are often found along the east side of the Continental Divide in summer and fall, from Black Mountain to Granite Butte and north to the Flesher Pass area. Additionally, elk are scattered east of State Highway 279 and the Continental Divide to Wolf Creek and the Missouri River/Holter Lake.

Where to Hunt

With the exception of the Bull Mountain area, access points to public lands in this region are very numerous. In addition to the major routes described in this chapter, expect to find many branch roads and trails that lead to more remote areas. Also, block management participation by landowners in some districts opens considerable private acreage to public hunting.

Bull Mountain

Along the west side of Bull Mountain, State Highway 399 (Whitetail Creek Road) runs through the Deerlodge National Forest for about four miles on the northwest side. To reach Highway 399, veer south from State Highway 69 about one mile south of Boulder. Hunting is possible to the east from Highway 399, but it's a hit-or-miss proposition for elk, with more misses likely than hits.

On the east side of Bull Mountain, Dunn Canyon Road (FR 510) springs from the west side of Highway 69 about twenty-two miles south of Boulder, where it passes through private land before reaching the national forest. This central portion of Bull Mountain is a checkerboard of NF and private land, which requires hunters to be very vigilant regarding property

Table 16-1 Bull Mountain

	Low	Moderate	High	Very High
Elk Numbers		•		
Hunters Per Square Mile			•	
Hunters Per Elk			•	
Trophy Potential	•			
Remote/Roadless Areas	•			

boundaries. On the bright side, there are currently several block management areas on the east side of Bull Mountain in the Dunn Canyon area that provide good access for elk hunting. If you're determined to take a bull, try to arrange an opening day hunt or wait until the snow flies. At this writing, antlerless tags for HD 370 (Bull Mountain) go begging. If you're looking for meat, draw one of these licenses and use it on block management land—the cooperating ranchers will appreciate it, as area elk are a little too friendly toward alfalfa fields and haystacks.

Boulder Mountains—South of Highway 12

Between I-15 and I-90 east of Butte, access to the Deerlodge National Forest is possible from all sides. On the south, FR 222 makes a loop north of I-90 in the Delmoe Lake area. Access this route from exit 233 on I-90 at Homestake Pass or from exit 241 at Pipestone Hot Springs. Expect to see lots of motor vehicles buzzing about in this area, particularly on the east side north of Pipestone. Hunt on foot in the rough canyons that are impassable to vehicle travel.

On the east side, FR 637 and FR 86 branch from Highway 399 (Whitetail Creek Road) south of Boulder. FR 86 heads southwest less than one mile south of Highway 399's intersection with Highway 69 south of Boulder. This route runs a dozen miles or so along the Little Boulder River. FR 637 is found about ten miles south of Highway 69, west of Highway 399. Less than a mile jaunt leads to public land and other branch roads. The best hunting in this area is found in isolated

Numerous roads and hunting pressure push elk into the timber in the Boulder Mountains. The author dropped this young bull in a thick stand of lodgepole pine.

pockets away from vehicle travel that have a water source, a secure bedding area, and something for elk to eat.

From the west, numerous routes into this portion of the Boulder Mountains spring from I-15 north of Butte—just drive the freeway and watch for national forest access signs. No matter how you reach public lands, hunt on foot away from vehicles but don't expect too much in the way of solitude, as there are lots of roads, trails, and hunters who like to use them.

North of I-15 and I-90 to Highway 12, roads abound on the Helena and Deerlodge National Forests. At present, the MDFWP estimates that less than 5 percent of elk habitat on public land is further than one mile from lands open to motorized travel. Lack of escape areas for bull elk is clearly reflected in typical population and harvest patterns. East of the Continental Divide, post-season bull-to-one-hundred-cows ratios drop as low as 5:100, some of the lowest in the state. West of the divide ratios run about 10:100. Statistics regarding when bulls are killed during the general season give an even more startling picture of the animals' inability to elude hunters in this highly roaded territory. On the average, about half of the bull elk killed fall in the first week of the season. If you plan to hunt later, expect to see plenty of ears but few antlers.

In the southern portion of this region, a major access route winds along the upper reaches of the Boulder River. FR 82 (Boulder River Road) heads west of I-15 at exit 151. This route crosses the Continental Divide between the Boulder and Clark Fork River, winding down Peterson Creek to intersect I-90 at exit 187 near Deer Lodge. From this road, many spur routes run north and south. Of particular note is FR 1572, which heads north along Thunderbolt Creek about eight miles west of I-15. This road ends at trail 65, which leads toward Electric Peak—one of the few roadless areas in the region. However tempting it is to drive the back roads and idle along open parks or logged areas, pinpoint timbered sidehills that provide a refuge from casual hunters—that's where you'll find the elk.

The midsection of the Boulder Mountains, the region south of Elliston on Highway 12 to Basin on I-15, is easily approached via Little Blackfoot River Road on the north or FR 172 along Basin Creek from the south. To reach Little Blackfoot River Road, motor south of Highway 12

Table 16-2 Boulder Mountains South

	Low	Moderate	High	Very High
Elk Numbers		●		
Hunters Per Square Mile			●	
Hunters Per Elk			●	
Trophy Potential	●			
Remote/Roadless Areas	●			

about one mile east of Elliston. This route forks about three miles from the highway; FR 227 veers southwest along the Little Blackfoot River, while FR 495 heads up Telegraph Creek. Both routes and their branches lead to good elk habitat. From Kading Campground on FR 227, trail 329 launches toward the Blackfoot Meadows and an unroaded area at the headwaters of the Little Blackfoot River. From the south, look for FR 172 just north of Basin. This route climbs toward the Basin Creek–Little Blackfoot divide. About five miles from Basin, a couple patches of somewhat secluded country are found east and west of the road. Another remote area is found along the top of the drainage divide near Bison Mountain.

Another area of note is found along the Rimini Road (FR 695), which runs south of Highway 12 about nine miles west of Helena. An uphill hike toward Black Mountain or Colorado Mountain leads to an area of roadless habitat to the east, with a smaller unroaded section to the west. Try these spots later in the season, as pressure from more accessible vicinities encourages animals to hole up away from the roads.

Boulder Mountains (North of Highway 12)

North of Highway 12 to Rogers Pass and the Blackfoot River, elk habitat forms something of a {T}, with the top of the letter formed by the mountains along the Continental Divide and the leg representing the continuous ridge that runs west of the divide between Nevada Creek and the Blackfoot River. A number of roads cross these mountains (I'm still calling them the Boulder Mountains for convenience, though they may not be named at all on a map) at various intervals, yielding abundant access options for elk hunting.

Just north of Highway 12, Priest Pass Road (FR335) wanders west up Sweeny Creek about nine miles west of Helena, crosses the Continental Divide, then drops into Dog Creek. East of the divide, this road provides access to about twenty square miles of public land in the Helena National Forest.

North of Mullan Pass, FR 136 launches east of State Highway 141 roughly three miles north of Avon. Near the Continental Divide, FR 136D branches north of FR 136, leading to trail 337. This trail departs north, accessing remote elk habitat in the Nevada Mountain vicinity.

From the east, it's also possible to reach essentially the same area via FR 485. To locate this road, head west from State Highway 279 at Canyon Creek on Little Prickly Pear Road (RD 707). About five miles west, watch for FR 485, which veers north. As the road nears the top of the Continental Divide look for FR 485D, which reaches trails 467 and 440 after about one mile. Trail 440 heads south along the Continental Divide, yielding access to a fair-size roadless area in the headwaters of Nevada Creek—good hunting for the solitude seeker. Trail 467 runs west along the Divide between Nevada Creek and the Blackfoot River, where elk like to hide in the isolated creek bottoms and basins.

Further west, FR 1163 winds over the Nevada Creek–Blackfoot River divide between Highway 141 and Highway 200. From the south, look for this road about five miles south of Helmville on Highway 141. Spur roads branch from this main route but are closed to motorized travel during the general elk season. Public land extends but a short distance west of FR 1163, so concentrate your efforts to the east.

South of Lincoln on Highway 200, Stemple Pass Road (RD 601) winds along Poorman Creek, crosses the Continental Divide at Stemple Pass, then descends to Highway 279 about eight miles north of Canyon Creek. This road offers many venues for elk hunting. During archery season or the early part of the general season, hunt pockets and ridges along the divide. If snow blows in, shift your attention to lower portions of the national forest both east and west of the divide. North of Stemple Pass, FR 1827 is closed to motorized travel after October 15 but offers a handy path into a considerable section of backcountry elk habitat.

Of particular note in this region is the area east of Highway 279 to the Missouri River that forms HD 339. Managed with special regulations, general hunting for bulls is restricted to spikes only. All hunting for brow-tined bulls requires a special license. Although odds of pulling this tag run less than 10 percent, it still offers better prospects than many other trophy areas in the state. Public-land hunting is limited, but there is some possibility on national forest and state land east of the Continental Divide in the Flesher Pass area, with public access from Highway 279. Additionally, several large block management properties offer elk hunting in HD 339. Along with the either-sex licenses that allow the taking of a brow-tined bull, antlerless tags are also issued through a drawing and

Table 16-3 Boulder Mountains North

	Low	Moderate	High	Very High
Elk Numbers			●	
Hunters Per Square Mile			●	
Hunters Per Elk			●	
Trophy Potential^	●			
Remote/Roadless Areas		●		

^ Very high in HD 339; special tag required.

often go begging. Ranchers enrolled in the block management program like to see cow hunters—take an antlerless elk to enjoy excellent eating, and sweeten landowner-hunter relations.

Hunting Strategies

If you're looking to kill a bull in this region with a rifle, hunt early. About half of the antlered animals harvested in the general season fall in the first week of the season, stacking the odds in favor of those who can devote several days to hunting on the front end.

Two factors drive this trend toward early harvest: the glut of roads in the region and hunting pressure, which is especially high during the first week of the season. These characteristics force elk to stay on the move or hole up in places where they're least likely to be bothered. Veteran hunters capitalize on these influences in a number of ways.

If you're familiar with an area or can devote a couple of days to scouting just prior to the season, locate a particular herd of animals that you can hunt at daylight on opening day. I say "daylight" because it's almost a sure bet that if you don't find them within an hour of shooting light, someone else will. This likely means a hike in the dark before dawn, but that bit of extra effort might have you notching your tag twenty minutes into the elk season.

Another very useful strategy in highly roaded regions during times of peak hunting pressure is to ambush elk along escape routes. Ridges, established game trails, and routes around natural barriers such as cliffs and boulder fields are excellent places to watch for wapiti as they move away from other hunters. Additionally, fingers of timber between meadows, clear-cuts, and burned hillsides are favored by fleeing elk. I once encountered dozens of elk in several small herds moving through a stand of timber below a prominent ridge while other hunters on foot and horseback pounded the pines along a trail above.

Although some brow-tined bulls remain with cow herds throughout the fall, biology and hunting pressure usually prompt older males to lead solitary lives or form bachelor bands of a few animals. In this region, use this knowledge when you hunt later in the year. If you encounter tracks of a herd of thirty animals wandering through the snow, there may be a brow-tined bull in the bunch, but it's just as likely that it's a large band of cows and spikes. If, however, you find two or three adult elk traveling together, hit their trail, as it may be a group of bachelor bulls. As you track them, watch for further indications of their sex. Bulls will rub their antlers long after the rut but usually aren't as enthusiastic about demolishing a sapling. I always look for bits of shredded bark or small rubs when tracking elk through the timber, as they clearly betray the presence of a bull.

Given the high mortality of bulls in this region due to hunting, most legal males are two-and-a-half-year-old animals. If you're at all interested in archery hunting, you'll find more bulls available during bow season than later in the general season. Young bulls often respond enthusiastically to bugling and cow calls, making them excellent quarry for novice archers. Some of the most enjoyable hunting in this region awaits those who can be afield on weekdays during archery season, when there are fewer humans about and bulls bugling in the pines.

17

SOUTHERN BITTERROOT, SAPPHIRE, ANACONDA MOUNTAINS

--------------◆--------------

Geographical Overview

The three mountain ranges that supply water to the Bitterroot River form this region. To the west, the Bitterroot Range juts sharply above the Bitterroot Valley to the Montana-Idaho divide. To the east, the lower, gentler slopes of the Sapphire Range mark an eighty-five-mile chain from Missoula south to the East Fork of the Bitterroot River. East of the Sapphires, the Anaconda Range runs northeast from Chief Joseph Pass, lending the water from its southwestern segment to the Bitterroot River's East Fork.

Of these ranges, the Bitterroot Mountains are the highest and possess some wickedly canted terrain. Typical topography consists of deep, east-west-running creek bottoms hemmed in on both sides by steep, heavily timbered hillsides. The ridges between these canyonlike valleys tend to narrow. Good elk habitat is often limited to small basins below the ridgetops and hanging valleys just under the Montana-Idaho divide. The Selway-Bitterroot Wilderness dominates public land in the mountains, where wheeled-vehicle travel is prohibited but an extensive trail system provides a multitude of travel options for folks on foot or horseback. Recent fire activity has reduced forest density in places, resulting in better forage production and stimulating the growth of deciduous shrubs highly palatable to elk.

On the east side of the Bitterroot Valley, the Sapphire Range parallels the Bitterroot River, its name reflecting area gemstones. Compared to the Bitterroot

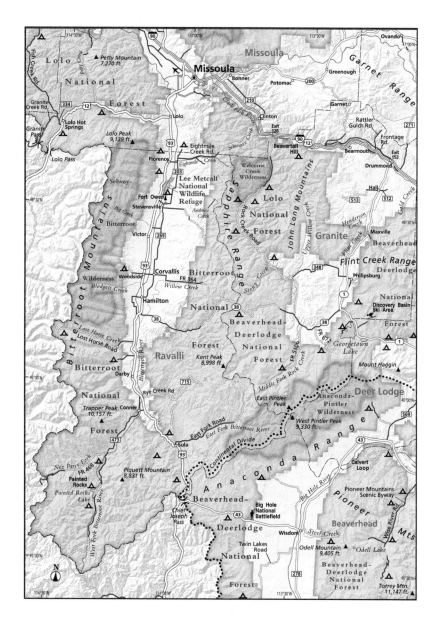

Range, the Sapphire Mountains are more productive elk habitat. Their undulating slopes are timbered but broken with meadows and grasslands, providing good winter and summer range for a host of big-game animals. One small designated wilderness area (Welcome Creek) graces the Sapphires, with several other roadless areas providing good elk hunting in backcountry settings. In 2000 extensive wildfires burned in the Sapphires,

Major wildlifes burned the Sapphire Mountains in the past two decades. A few years after the blaze, these are excellent places to find elk.

especially in the south, creating temporary difficulties for elk and other ungulates but ultimately improving thousands of acres of habitat.

The Anaconda Range isn't as popular with recreationists as many other areas, but its high country is some of the most wild and beautiful in the state. Toward the north end, numerous peaks rise beyond ten thousand feet. The interior of the range is home to the Anaconda-Pintler Wilderness. Several roadless areas abut this designated wilderness, producing large expanses of unspoiled landscape. Forested slopes give way to open basins and ridges near timberline, with enough meadows and grassy parklands to provide ideal summer range for elk.

Elk Distribution

Elk distribution in the Bitterroot Range is fairly easy to describe. Animals winter in the Bitterroot Valley, primarily near the boundary between private lands and the Bitterroot National Forest. Wapiti summer at high-elevations along the Montana-Idaho border, with some exchange of elk occurring between the two states in summer and fall. Growing herds of nonmigratory animals are building in the valley, such as those that frequent the foothills between Blodgett and Roaring Lion creeks west of Hamilton. Heavy concentrations of wintering elk are located west of Victor in the Sweathouse Creek drainage and west of Stevensville between Big Creek and Kootenai Creek.

Toward the southern end of the Bitterroots, migrating elk from the uplands of the West Fork and Nez Perce Fork of the Bitterroot River drift into the valley near the confluence of those streams to pass the winter. Because of the remote nature of the habitat and strenuous hunting conditions, around one in four bulls taken from the Bitterroots sports at least six points on one antler—one of the highest ratios in the state for areas without special hunting regulations geared toward trophy bulls.

Sapphire Mountain wapiti move to lower elevations to winter, although mild years may find them well up in the mountains throughout the entire hunting season. Elk numbers tend to increase as one moves south in the Sapphires, though populations north of the Ambrose Creek drainage east of Stevensville increased notably around the dawning of the twenty-first century. Although bull-to-cow ratios aren't exceptionally high, a reasonably high percentage of the antlered-animal harvest consists of bulls with six or more points on one antler.

Like other high, rugged mountainous areas in the state, elk favor the uplands of the Anaconda Range during the summer and fall, then retreat to lower slopes and foothills during the winter. On the north end, wintering wapiti concentrate southwest of Anaconda on the lower slopes of Mount Haggin and the foothills in the Mill Creek and French Creek drainages. Animals also drift into the Big Hole Valley east of the mountains, but south of the Pintler Peaks vicinity most elk that summer along the eastern flank of the Anaconda Range actually migrate over the Continental Divide to winter on the East Fork of the Bitterroot River toward Sula. The East Fork/Sula area also picks up animals that descend from the headwaters of the East Fork near the Bitterroot River–Rock Creek divide. North of this divide, elk from the Anaconda Range often move into the lower portions of the Middle Fork and East Fork of Rock

Creek. As a general rule, elk numbers increase somewhat from north to south, depending on winter severity and the condition of summer range. The warmer months find animals high in the mountains within the Anaconda-Pintler Wilderness, where they'll stay until severe weather or the migratory urge moves them toward their wintering grounds.

Where to Hunt

From areas with numerous drive-through loop routes to wilderness basins miles from the nearest road, there's a destination to suit any hunting style in this region. No matter where you prowl, significant snowfall can drastically alter travel conditions and elk distribution, so it's essential to match your hunting plans with current conditions.

Southern Bitterroot Mountains

From Lolo Pass on the north to the headwaters of the West Fork of the Bitterroot River on the south, this portion of the Bitterroot Mountains is dominated by the Selway-Bitterroot Wilderness. However, non-wilderness lands with vehicle access are found along a strip south of U.S. Highway 12, along the east face of the mountains in the Bitterroot Valley and to the south in the Nez Perce Fork and West Fork drainages of the Bitterroot River.

South of Highway 12, Plum Creek Timber (PCT) lands mingle with national forest. This area has high road densities, although many spur roads have year-long or seasonal closures, making them useful travel routes for elk hunting. Three main roads branch from Highway 12: FR 451 is found about eleven miles west of Lolo, FR 37 about twenty-one miles west of Lolo, and FR 461 about thirty miles west of Lolo. Use these routes, which have variable travel restrictions, to penetrate elk habitat in this area, then hunt the saddles and creek bottoms away from the roads.

In the Selway-Bitterroot Wilderness, nearly every major creek bottom is associated with a trail. Trails also cross many of the drainage divides near the summit of the range along the Idaho border. Rather than attempt to describe in detail any portion of this trail system, here are some observations for wilderness hunters, assuming that anyone seriously planning a

Much of the good elk habitat in the Bitterroot Mountains is far from a trailhead. A riding horse and pack mule makes it much easier on the back and legs.

backcountry hunt possesses good map skills and a thorough understanding of elk habitat.

Elk roam throughout the wilderness portion of the Bitterroots but favor high-country basins and ridges, where there's more forage and it's easier to travel than in the dense stands of timber on the steep slopes. However, animals also hole up in some heavily forested areas, especially on gentler inclines where deciduous shrubs or small clearings provide a food base.

With a good topographical map, aided with current satellite and Internet mapping tools, if you have them, it's possible to pinpoint basins, ridgetops, and hillsides that exhibit the type of terrain most suitable to elk. Choose a hunting destination based on these factors, but give yourself some flexibility to move in case elk aren't currently using your chosen area.

West of U.S. Highway 93, about nine miles north of Darby, one notable exclusion to the wilderness portion of the Bitterroot Range occurs in the Lost Horse Creek drainage. Lost Horse Road (FR 429) winds some twenty miles up Lost Horse Creek, terminating at the Schumaker and

Bear Creek Pass campgrounds near the Montana-Idaho divide. Enterprising hunters can make archery and early general-season forays, depending on the weather, along the divide into drainages to the north and south of this road.

On the southern portion of the Bitterroot Range, two major roads offer access to quality elk habitat in the Nez Perce Fork and West Fork drainages of the Bitterroot River. From Highway 93 about six miles south of Darby, State Highway 473 (West Fork Road) heads up the West Fork of the Bitterroot River. Some fifteen miles up the river, FR 468 (Nez Perce Road) veers west up the Nez Perce Fork. Highway 473 continues up the West Fork to Painted Rocks Lake. Beyond the lakes the route winds for nearly twenty miles before reaching the Montana-Idaho divide. Similarly, FR 468 runs about fifteen miles from the West Fork Road before cresting the divide at Nez Perce Pass.

Numerous spur roads with various travel restrictions branch along the first ten miles or so of Nez Perce Road, with good hunting possibilities. As the route approaches Nez Perce Pass, large expanses of roadless territory lie north and south of the road where elk hunters travel cross-country or via several established trails. This country beckons bowhunters, where September is often just right for hiking and hunting, and the bugles of rutting bulls makes them easier to find.

Beyond Painted Rocks Lake, similar access options await elk hunters in the West Fork drainage. Spur roads branch from West Fork Road with various travel restrictions. Some seven miles from the Montana-Idaho

Table 17-1 Southern Bitterroot Mountains

	Low	Moderate	High	Very High
Elk Numbers*		●		
Hunters Per Square Mile		●		
Hunters Per Elk		●		
Trophy Potential*		●		
Remote/Roadless Areas				●

* Elk populations and trophy potential are higher toward the south.

divide, West Fork Road branches, with FR 5669 heading west up Woods Creek and West Fork Road (FR 091) continuing south. Backcountry hunting possibilities abound north of FR 5669 and south of FR 091 as one nears the divide. The entire stretch of country between Woods Creek Pass and the Nez Perce Fork is roadless—an appealing destination for hunters looking to leave civilization in the rearview mirror. East of Painted Rocks Lake, another sprawling expanse of roadless territory is found from the West Fork drainage to Highway 93. Trail 55 just west of Painted Rocks Lake on FR 1130 offers one feasible route into this area, or head out cross-country from one of the roads.

Sapphire Mountains

Numerous roads crisscross the northern end of the Sapphire Range, which consists of intermingled national forest, PCT, and state lands. Some roads are open to yearlong travel; others are closed or governed by seasonal restrictions.

From the east side FR 502 offers numerous access options in the Swartz Creek drainage. From I-90 take exit 121 west at Clinton. Follow the frontage road south about two miles to FR 502, which turns up Swartz Creek. This route winds all the way to the top of the Bitterroot River–Clark Fork River divide, with many branch roads (travel restrictions may apply) fanning from this main corridor. Easy access and proximity to Missoula mean plenty of hunting pressure. Solitude is in somewhat greater supply just to the south in the Welcome Creek Wilderness Area. Trails into this small wilderness are found along Rock Creek Road south of exit 126 on I-90. Trail 179 departs about nine miles from the interstate on the west side of the road at Sawmill Creek. Trail 225 heads up Welcome Creek approximately eight miles further down the road. Although these paths lead into a designated wilderness area, expect to see hikers on the trails. Hunting prospects are best away from the trails during midweek.

South of the Welcome Creek Wilderness, a considerable block of roadless land lies on the east side of the Sapphires from Bear Creek to the Stony Creek area. North of Alder Creek, numerous roads crisscross the slopes, but these are currently closed to wheeled, motorized vehicles. About seven miles south of the Welcome Creek trailhead, Wahlquist

Trailhead (trail 233) offers good access to the area. Another ten miles up the road, Sandstone/Wyman Trailhead launches trails 1269 and 226. Look for good archery hunting in out-of-the-way pockets in this vicinity, with fine prospects for hunting the early portion of the general season as well.

On the west side of the Sapphires, north of the Burnt Fork of the Bitterroot River, private land generally runs within a mile or two of the Bitterroot River–Rock Creek divide, yielding limited opportunity for public hunting. One notable exception to this is the state-owned Three Mile Wildlife Management Area. To reach this area, head east on State Highway 203 from Highway 93 about eight miles north of Stevensville. About five miles after the highway turns south, turn onto Three Mile Creek Road (FR 640). This road jogs alternately west and north, reaching the WMA about nine miles from Highway 203. Hunt south of the road onto the WMA or scout the PCT lands to the northeast.

Further south, Willow Creek Road (FR 364) runs east of State Highway 269 at Corvallis. The road reaches the Bitterroot National Forest boundary about eight miles from Corvallis, then continues another two miles or so to trail 300. Take this trail up Willow Creek into remote country to the east, or drive one of the spur roads that wander north and south of FR 364 a bit before the trailhead.

South of Hamilton about four miles, Skalkaho Road (State Highway 38) runs over the Sapphire Range, connecting with Highway 1 northwest of Georgetown Lake. This "highway" (a fair amount of it is rough gravel) offers numerous possibilities for elk hunters on both the east and west side of the mountains. Hunting can be good from Skalkaho Road itself, or take one of many branch roads that lead to more remote locations on either side of the Bitterroot River–Rock Creek divide.

The East Fork of the Bitterroot River marks the southern end of the Sapphire Range. Two major routes lead into the southern Sapphires: Rye Creek Road and East Fork Road. Rye Creek Road (FR 75) runs east of Highway 93 about twenty-three miles south of Hamilton. A drive of around six miles leads to the national forest boundary. The road winds and climbs almost to the crest of the range, then turns north, and eventually connects with Skalkaho Road. Many branch roads, some with vehicle restrictions, spring from this wandering route, offering a myriad of hunting options. Where the road reaches the Rye Creek–Martin Creek

Table 17-2 Sapphire Mountains

	Low	Moderate	High	Very High
Elk Numbers		●		
Hunters Per Square Mile			●	
Hunters Per Elk			●	
Trophy Potential		●		
Remote/Roadless Areas			●	

divide, a large, roadless area in the upper Martin Creek drainage beckons to the east. Similarly, East Fork Road (State Highway 472, FR 432 . . . whew!) runs east from Sula on Highway 93. This route ends at trail 168, which heads up Moose Creek about twenty miles from Sula. There's inviting roadless country in the Moose Creek drainage, or take one of the branch routes that run north of East Fork Road; some are closed during the elk season, yielding good hike-in hunting.

Anaconda Range

The western end of the Anaconda Range can be accessed from Highway 93. Just east of the highway, a sizeable block of roadless territory awaits in the Reimel and Tolan Creek drainages. About three miles south of Sula on Highway 93, look for FR 727, which leads to trails 78 and 175, roughly two and four miles from the highway. Hunt to the west in high basins and drainage heads along the Continental Divide.

A little further east, look for good access from East Fork Road (described above with the Sapphire Mountains). About seven miles from Sula, FR 5753 climbs into the mountains on the south side of the road, crosses a drainage divide, then loops back to East Fork Road along Meadow Creek as FR 725. Various spur roads with travel restrictions during the general elk season spring from this route, making it an ideal area for drive/hike hunting with miles of easy walking on gated roads.

Toward the end of East Fork Road, several trails launch toward the Anaconda-Pintler Wilderness. About two miles south of the road on FR

724, trail 433 heads up the East Fork of the Bitterroot River, climbing to the Continental Divide on the spine of the Anaconda Range (via trail 313), where it intersects the Continental Divide Trail (trail 9). It's around thirteen miles to the top of the divide, but numerous ravines and ridges offer good hunting from lower on the trail.

To reach the northern portion of the Anaconda Range, you'll need to travel south from Philipsburg. Some access is possible south of George-town Lake, but two roads provide more options from Highway 38 (Skalkaho Road). The first of these is FR 672, which follows the East Fork of Rock Creek about six miles south of Highway 1. The second is FR 5106, which parallels the Middle Fork of Rock Creek another three miles down the highway. Both of these routes wind several miles through private land before reaching the National Forest. Each road sports branch routes on their lower reaches. Both also terminate at trails leading into the Anaconda-Pintler Wilderness, offering various options for easy access versus remote hunting.

From the south side, access to the Anaconda Mountains springs from the Big Hole Valley. The typical land-management pattern involves roaded areas at lower elevations, ending at the boundary of the Anaconda-Pintler Wilderness. On the west end, FR 1203 snakes into the mountains from State Highway 43, about fourteen miles west of Wisdom. This road and its branches compose a well-tracked region where some spur routes are closed to vehicles during the general hunting season. About sixteen miles north of Wisdom on State Highway

Table 17-3 Anaconda Range

	Low	Moderate	High	Very High
Elk Numbers		●		
Hunters Per Square Mile			●	
Hunters Per Elk		●		
Trophy Potential		●		
Remote/Roadless Areas			●	

278, FR 185 heads west approximately ten miles to the Pintler Lake area. This route leads to two trails not far beyond the lake, 127 and 37. About a mile before the lake, FR 1278 branches west, leading to trail 369. Each of these trails leads into Anaconda-Pintler Wilderness and high-country hunting toward the Continental Divide. Similar travel routes are also found another six miles north on Highway 278 at FR 1223.

Hunting Strategies

In the Bitterroot and Anaconda ranges, elk herds are primarily migratory. Archery hunters and those toting a rifle in mild weather during the general season should focus on high elevation ridges and basins at the top of drainage divides. Snowfall drives animals to lower elevations, but early snows of only several inches typically have little affect on elk.

Many migratory elk herds tend to inhabit a particular band of elevation. If you find animals on ridgetops at eight thousand feet in one drainage, chances are very high that elk are hanging at similar elevations in the next drainage. If you're not finding elk at high elevations during archery season or the beginning weeks of the general season, drop a bit lower. If animals are few at low elevations later on, move up. Once you've found the preferred elevation band, hunt along this contour, as that's where the majority of animals should be found.

Compared to many other places, bull harvest is spread more evenly throughout the season in this region. Hunting is almost always good on opening day, but the surprise element of early hunting pressure doesn't claim as large a proportion of elk. While most antlered bulls that fall to elk stalkers in this region are young animals, a notable percentage carry six or more points on at least one antler. Many people assume that the first week of the general season is the best time to hunt a big-antlered bull, but conditions may actually favor trophy hunters later in the fall. Tracking snow and heavier concentrations of animals at lower elevations, provided they don't hole up on private land, yield excellent prospects for finding older bulls. If you're targeting a wallhanger in this region, be patient. Archers also have good potential here for trophy hunting on a general elk tag—those who make the extra effort to find secluded areas away from other hunters tend to find more vocal (and bigger) bulls.

Significant fires have burned thousands and thousands of acres in this region over the past couple of decades. These events typically result in excellent elk habitat one to four years after the fires and beyond. If little cover is left on a burn, elk often utilize the edges. In areas where they're relatively undisturbed, though, wapiti may graze and bed in the middle of a large burn where there's little apparent cover.

If you hunt the burns, it's essential to understand that as the roots of seared trees begin to rot, they become increasingly unstable. High winds may topple weakened trees, so hunt elsewhere in a howling gale. Additionally, never pitch a camp or tether horses within falling range of scorched timber. Once burned trees hit the ground, an obstacle course of other-worldly proportions is often the result. Humans avoid these tangles like the plague, but elk don't. Wapiti step easily over fallen timber and will casually traverse miles of deadfall. If you're willing to do a little high-stepping yourself, you may find yourself among herds of elk that you'll have all to yourself.

18

FLINT CREEK, JOHN LONG, GARNET MOUNTAINS

------------♦------------

Geographical Overview

Unless you're quite familiar with Montana geography, you probably haven't heard of the Flint Creek, John Long, or Garnet mountains. If you've driven I-90 between Butte and Missoula, though, you've seen them all. The Flint Creek Mountains dominate the skyline west of Deer Lodge, where one stony peak, Mount Powell, rises beyond ten thousand feet. Where the Clark Fork River pinches between the mountains between Bearmouth and Rock Creek, the John Long Mountains shadow its course to the south, while the slopes of the Garnet Range rise to the north.

Of the three ranges, the Flint Creek Mountains are the highest and most rugged. Extending about twenty-five miles from north to south and twenty miles from east to west, the highest peaks in the Flint Creek range are found to the east. Numerous lakes dot these mountains in open meadows and among the timber. In general, this area is well watered and receives considerable snowpack—evidenced by the presence of the Discovery Basin Ski Area tucked away near Phillipsburg. The majority of this range is found within the Deerlodge National Forest with abundant access for elk hunting on public land. Road densities tend toward the heavy side, a result of past mining activity.

West of the Flint Creek range, the John Long Mountains mark the divide between the Phillipsburg Valley (Flint Creek) and Rock Creek. These mountains aren't particularly high (few summits top seventy-five hundred feet), but they are quite steep and rugged in places. The southern end of this unheralded range lies toward the upper reaches of Rock Creek, where the terrain tends to be more open than the north, creating excellent elk habitat. Good access for hunting occurs in the northern and central portions of the John Long Mountains on the Deerlodge National Forest, but the southern segment of the range is dominated by private land.

North of I-90, the Garnet Mountains sprawl haphazardly along a considerable stretch of country from Bonner to Avon, covering about sixty miles from east to west. Though classified as part of the same mountains, the portion of the Garnets east of Drummond and Douglas Creek are somewhat separate from the rest of the range. For the most part, the Garnets sport moderate elevation (five thousand to seven thousand feet)

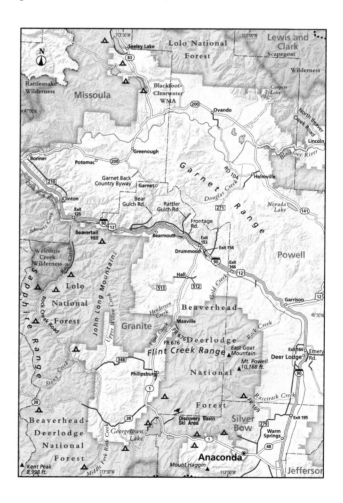

Remote country in the John Long Mountains is the best place to look for a large-antlered elk.

and are quite heavily timbered, although logging and fire activity has greatly reduced the forest in places.

Of significance to elk hunters is the fact that none of the Garnet Range is national forest, although a considerable amount of public land is available under the purview of the BLM and state. Major private holdings are owned by the Plum Creek Timber Company that extensively manages its property for forest production. Plum Creek Timber has historically opened its lands to hunting—a generous gesture many elk hunters take for granted and some abuse. Although the company closed many roads to motorized travel in the mid-1990s, illegal travel by ATVs for hunting and recreation is an ongoing problem in the Garnet Mountains, not only on Plum Creek Timber lands but BLM and state areas as well.

Elk Distribution

Elk numbers essentially doubled in the Flint Creek Range from 1985 to 2005 but have stabilized somewhat since that time, yielding robust populations throughout these mountains. Large numbers winter in the Lost Creek and Racetrack drainages north of Anaconda. Similarly, wintering elk occupy most of the foothills in the Deer Lodge Valley south and west of I-90 from Racetrack Creek to Flint Creek. Animals also pass the cold months in the Phillipsburg Valley. Most elk from these wintering grounds head for the high country come spring, dispersing over the entire mountain range during the summer and fall.

In general, elk numbers are higher toward the southern end of the Flint Creek Range than the north. Animals find "elk refuges" on private lands in the southern foothills during the fall, where up to 70 percent of the elk associated with the southern portion of these mountains may congregate if early winter weather pushes them to lower elevations during the general season. Although overall elk counts are higher to the south, the northern section of the Flint Creek Mountains maintains a slightly higher percentage of bulls in the population, likely due to more remote, roadless habitat where they encounter fewer hunters.

Elk distribution in the John Long Mountains is comparable to that in the Flint Creek Range. Small herds are found at high elevations during the summer, while animals band into larger groups in the foothills and valleys (primarily the Rock Creek and Flint Creek drainages) during the winter. Overall numbers are a bit higher in the southern portion of these mountains southeast of Upper Willow Creek, as many elk are insulated from hunting pressure on private lands. Although the John Longs (not to be confused with long johns) are close enough to Butte and Missoula to receive considerable hunting pressure, ample cover and remote territory allow a reasonable percentage of bulls to achieve the six-point status coveted by horn hunters.

North of I-90, elk are found throughout the Garnet Mountains. Given the high percentage of private land in this area, elk frequent ranchlands not only during the winter but in the summer and fall as well. Particularly high numbers roam the Douglas Creek drainage north of Drummond where a few "refuge" ranches closed to hunting thwart hunter harvest and keep elk numbers artificially high—much to the chagrin of neighboring outfits that would like to see fewer animals raiding alfalfa fields and damaging fences.

Numerous elk are also found west of Helmville from Yourname Creek north to Dunigan Mountain. Animals are also abundant during the winter months and other times of the year in the Potomac Valley. Herds of these elk often ascend to higher elevations to the south during the summer and fall. Bands of wapiti are also scattered along the southern face of the Garnet Range above the Clark Fork River from Drummond to Missoula. However, an extensive wildfire in the Ryan Creek area in 2000 severely reduced cover for elk. Widespread logging activity on the west end of the Garnets has also reduced security for elk, making them more vulnerable to hunting pressure.

As a percentage of the overall herd, bulls represent a feeble portion of the population. In most locations in the Garnet Mountains, just around 7 percent of the animals observed in spring counts are bulls, one of the lower percentages in the state. However, in areas where elk have access to "refuge" ranches, as many as one in three animals may carry antlers.

Where to Hunt

Public land is available in all locations covered in this chapter, although the amount (and access) is lower in the Garnet Range than the John Long or Flint Creek mountains. Cooperation in the block management program by private landowners provides considerable opportunity for additional public hunting—nearing 150,000 acres some years—so it's definitely worth your time to research BM properties in addition to traditional public lands. In the Garnet Mountains, particularly the western portion, privately owned Plum Creek Timber holdings are typically open for public hunting as well. Respect the corporation's rules and road closures, as the company is under no obligation to allow public use of its lands.

Flint Creek Mountains

Approach to the Flint Creek Range along public routes is possible from all four directions of the compass, with many roads and trails fanning from several major access points. Boundaries between public and private lands are very irregular in places, so it's wise to carry maps that show property ownership should you find yourself hunting in transitional areas. In addition to the destinations described below, public hunting (archery only) is available on the Montana State Prison Ranch near Deer Lodge, where you'll mainly find cows, calves, and yearling (spike) bulls—check with Region 2 headquarters of the MDFWP in Missoula for details.

From the north, Gold Creek Road heads south of I-90 at exit 166. Just over four miles in, this route forks, with FR 636 veering west and FR 302 aiming south. Both of these routes offer drive-in access to the heavily roaded area on the northern end of the range. About three miles inside the Deerlodge National Forest Boundary, FR 302 passes along Pikes Peak Creek, providing access to a large roadless area to the south in the vicinity of Pikes Peak and Easy Goat Mountain.

On the northwest side, FR 707 runs along Douglas Creek east of State Highway 1 a little more than two miles south of Hall. This route hits a section of state land about five miles from the highway, then veers west through alternating sections of private and public land before reaching Douglas Creek Forest Service Cabin. About one mile beyond the cabin, FR 1544 forks to the south, providing access to several spur roads with seasonal closures during the general elk season. These are well worth a hunter's time, as they yield easy travel in some good habitat away from vehicle disturbance.

A bit further south on Highway 1, Maxville Road (FR 676) heads east from Maxville along Boulder Creek. Two trails into a roadless area in the Copper Creek Lakes and Boulder Lakes vicinity launch from this route. Trail 34 is located at the end of FR 1533, about eight miles from Highway 1 on FR 676. Slightly more than one mile beyond FR 1533, look for trail 36. The roadless, high-elevation character of this area commends itself to ambitious bowhunters or hunting during the early part of the general season.

From the southwest, FR 242 heads along the North Fork of Flint Creek from RD 65 (to Discovery Basin Ski Area) about two miles north of Highway 1 on the east side of Georgetown Lake. This route leads to the headwaters of Flint Creek's North Fork, then winds back west over the spine of the Flint Creek Range as FR 1525 toward Phillipsburg. North of the Discovery Basin Ski Area, a semi-remote stretch of habitat lies along the ridge between the North Fork of Flint Creek and Fred Burr Creek. At its high point in the Fred Burr Lake area, FR 242 yields good hike-in hunting in most directions via established trails or cross-country travel.

About eight miles east of Georgetown Lake on Highway 1, FR 195 runs north for about four miles to the beginning of trail 45, which follows Foster Creek. This route is worth remembering during the mid- to late weeks of the general season, when elk begin piling up to the east in the Lost Creek drainage.

On the eastern front, FR 169 opens up varied access options in the Racetrack Creek drainage. From I-90, head west from exit 195. Watch for signs to FR 169 and the Racetrack Campground. This route jogs west and south for a few miles, then lines out west along Modesty Creek before veering north to enter the Deerlodge National Forest about ten miles from I-90. Beyond the Racetrack Campground, FR 169 follows Racetrack Creek, then veers up its North Fork, ending about twelve miles later at trail 63. This trail offers access to the large roadless area to the north in the Easy Goat Mountain area, with cross-country travel toward high ridges possible to the east and west. Further down, don't overlook the semi-remote country in the Indian Meadows area, which is accessed via trail 56. Look for the best hunting in the timber, secluded basins and along remote ridges.

Further north, numerous routes to public land are found in the Rock Creek Lake area west of Deer Lodge. From I-90, take exit 184 west on the Business Loop into Deer Lodge. At West Milwaukee Street, head west. This street merges to the Old Stage Road just west of town. About eight miles from Deer Lodge, FR 168 runs west toward Rock Creek Lake. Look for two trailheads at Rock Creek Lake. Trail 115 leads to the Dolus Lakes vicinity just south of Pikes Peak. Trail 53 heads up Rock

Table 18-1 Flint Creek Mountains

	Low	Moderate	High	Very High
Elk Numbers		•		
Hunters Per Square Mile			•	
Hunters Per Elk			•	
Trophy Potential	•			
Remote/Roadless Areas		•		

Creek toward Easy Goat Mountain. Hunt the ridges north and south of these trails, where you'll find a fine measure of solitude and scenery.

John Long Mountains

As a percentage of total area, the John Long Mountains boast a large portion that is closed to motorized travel year-round or regulated with seasonal closures. Even though a Missoula hunter may travel less than an hour to reach these mountains, travel restrictions have done wonders for maintaining the elk herd. General license holders can kill any antlered elk (spikes included), as opposed to the brow-tined-bull regulations needed to ensure enough breeding males in the population in heavily roaded regions elsewhere. Although motorized restrictions are in place throughout much of the mountains, abundant points of public access make the "getting to" part of hunting the John Longs a simple proposition, except on the south-ern portion of the range that occurs primarily on private land.

From I-90, access to the highly traveled north end of the range is possible from the Beavertail Hill area. At exit 130, head south toward Beavertail Hill Campground. FR 354 heads into the mountains and the Lolo National Forest about four miles beyond the campground. The route climbs quickly via switchbacks toward the sixty-eight-hundred-foot summit of Strawberry Mountain. Numerous spur roads depart from FR 354, some of which carry travel restrictions during both the archery and general elk seasons. In the absence of established trails, these closed roads facilitate travel via foot or mountain bike. Look for heavy timber on the north-facing slopes in this area, except in logged areas. Huntable popula-tions of elk inhabit the north side of the John Longs, but numbers are generally higher to the south.

To the east, two major access routes launch from Highway 1. At Hall, Farm to Market Road heads west, reaching a {T} after about two miles. Head south on Lower Willow Creek Road, then watch for FR 358 about four miles later; this runs past Lower Willow Creek Reservoir. About five miles beyond the reservoir, the route hits the Lolo National Forest boundary. FR 358 continues north for several miles, but two branch roads veer south and east, eventually reaching segments of road with seasonal closures during hunting season. This is a good area for hunters who like the convenience of vehicle travel but are willing to hike a mile or more from their rigs.

About six miles south of Hall, Henderson Creek Road (FR 448) also begins west of Highway 1. A drive of about six miles takes you to the national forest boundary. From here, FR 448 swings south, winding some fifteen miles through NF and private lands before it reconnects with Highway 1 about two miles north of Phillipsburg. Many branch roads fan from FR 448 west of Henderson Mountain, yielding numerous options for vehicle travel.

Upper Willow Creek flows from north to south on the south side of the John Long Mountains, offering a natural travel route into the high country but also forming an important management boundary as well. From Upper Willow Creek west to Rock Creek lies the largest chunk of roadless elk habitat in the John Long Mountains.

From State Highway 348 (Rock Creek Road) about thirteen miles west of Phillipsburg, the Willow Creek Road (FR 88) heads up its namesake creek, reaching public lands (BLM and state) about seven miles from the highway. It then continues to the Deerlodge National Forest, where it winds another nine miles or so to the summit of Sandstone Ridge, which divides the Rock Creek and Upper Willow Creek watersheds. Hike-in hunting is possible east of this route in semi-remote country toward Black Pine Ridge. However, a strip of private land is found along the road, so make sure you're aware of property boundaries before heading out. Toward the summit of Sandstone Ridge, good hunting prospects via foot travel are found north and south of the road.

For backcountry hunters, the uplands of the John Long Mountains east of Rock Creek are the crown jewel of the range. Although roadless, several trails lead into the mountains from Rock Creek Road, yielding numerous options for travel. Additionally, this area can be approached from the Sandstone Ridge vicinity described above. Overall, this area is composed of steep slopes and jutting ridges. Travel on the trails isn't too bad, but cross-country jaunts can empty the lungs in a hurry.

To reach the major trailheads, take the Rock Creek Road south of I-90 at exit 126. Although graveled, Rock Creek Road receives much travel and is often viciously washboarded. About twelve miles south of the interstate, Grizzly Campground and trailhead are located just east of

Table 18-2 John Long Mountains

	Low	Moderate	High	Very High
Elk Numbers		•		
Hunters Per Square Mile			•	
Hunters Per Elk			•	
Trophy Potential		•		
Remote/Roadless Areas			•	

the road in the Ranch Creek drainage. Trail 65 departs up Ranch Creek; trail 208 heads up Grizzly Creek. About seven miles further south, Butte Cabin trailhead provides access to trail 224 and trail 227. Trail 224 parallels Butte Cabin Creek. Trail 227 follows a ridge to the north—but requires a nasty set of switchbacks to get there. Roughly a dozen miles beyond Butte Cabin, Hogback trailhead launches trail 268 north toward Hogback Ridge, yielding an attractive route to the upper reaches of numerous gulches and creeks favored by area elk. A couple of miles beyond Hogback, trail 228 departs the Sandstone trailhead, winding up a series of switchbacks on its march toward Sandstone Ridge. Along with access via these trails, cross-country hunting from Rock Creek Road puts an ambitious soul away from the crowds in a hurry.

Garnet Mountains

The primary venue for public hunting in the western portion of the Garnet Range occurs on Plum Creek Timber holdings and isolated parcels of state land. Before heading out, contact Plum Creek Timber Company's office in Missoula for travel information on their property. Isolated parcels of private land owned by individuals are found within Plum Creek (PCT) and state areas, so it's essential to navigate carefully while elk hunting to avoid trespassing.

From State Highway 200, Morrison Lane runs south near the post office at Potomac. This road heads up Arkansas Creek, reaching PCT lands about five miles from the highway. Other access points to PCT lands are possible along Highway 200 between Potomac and Bonner. Hunting opportunity also occurs on the south side of the range via Cramer Creek Road, which is found north of I-90 at exit 130. This route heads northeast, providing access to PCT and state lands on the south side of the mountains. Low habitat security and plenty of hunting pressure take a heavy toll on bulls in these areas—if you're aiming for antlers, it's wise to hunt early.

A bit further east, public access is plentiful in the Lubrecht State Experimental Forest and BLM lands in the vicinity of Garnet Ghost Town (a historical site). From the north, Garnet Back Country Byway heads south of Highway 200 about six miles east of Potomac. This route snakes through state land, where hunting opportunities are possible north of the road. About five miles from the highway, the road yields access to BLM, state, and PCT lands. From the south, this area may also be approached from Bear Gulch Road, which runs north of I-90 at Bearmouth. To reach this route, exit the interstate at Drummond (exit 153), then take the frontage road on the north side of the interstate west about eleven miles. Bear Gulch Road winds north into the mountains, through a mix of private, PCT, and BLM land, reaching the Garnet Ghost Town about eleven miles from the highway. In this vicinity, look

Proximity to Missoula and easy driving access create considerable pressure in the Garnet Mountains. Hunt early in the season for best odds on a bull.

Table 18-3 Garnet Mountains

	Low	Moderate	High	Very High
Elk Numbers			•	
Hunters Per Square Mile			•	
Hunters Per Elk		•		
Trophy Potential	•			
Remote/Roadless Areas	•			

for access to state, PCT, and BLM property in several directions. It's a popular destination with Missoulians but not the sort of place I'd target if traveling from afar.

A bit further east, good hunting is possible on BLM land in the Chamberlain Creek and Yourname Creek drainages. The primary access route into this area is Garnet National Recreation Trail, which is open to bicycle, horse, and foot travel. To reach this trail, head west on Ovando-Helmville Road (RD 104) from State Highway 271 at Helmville. About six miles from Helmville, watch for Wales Creek Road (RD 121). Take this route west about two miles to the BLM border, then another three miles or so to the beginning of the Garnet National Recreation Trail. Access is also possible from the north via the Scotty Brown Road (FR 2801, RD 110) south of Highway 200 about six miles west of Ovando. Elk numbers are quite high in this area, but early in the fall animals often flee to private lands, where they're insulated from hunting pressure.

East of Douglas Creek, another sizeable block of BLM land graces the Garnet Mountain highlands in the Hoodoo Mountain and Devil Mountain area. To access this area from the north, look for Cottonwood Meadow Road (RD 117, FR 2865) south of Highway 141 on the western end of Nevada Lake. This route runs west about one mile, then swings south just before Braziel Creek. It then runs about three miles south before reaching BLM lands. From the south, take RD 16, which runs along Brock Creek from exit 170 on I-90. Elk habitat is excellent in this area, with good hunting prospects. If hunting pressure becomes intense, though, many animals head toward surrounding private lands.

Hunting Strategies

Although the Flint Creek Range has sections of roadless land where elk enjoy reasonable security, nearly one in two bulls taken in the general season fall in the first week. If you're hunting an easily accessed area, the first week, especially the first two days, is the optimal time to find a bull. A number of hunters have expressed concern with this trend to the MDFWP, indicating that they'd like to see more mature bulls in the elk population. Nonetheless, the Flint Creek Range still kicks out some older bulls—in recent years around 10 percent of the antlered animals killed sported six tines on at least one antler.

If you're set on finding a big one in these mountains, plan to put in some miles to find pockets of overlooked habitat away from roads. Although formally designated roadless areas are ideal places to start, outfitter camps or easy trail access can put significant hunting pressure in certain backcountry locales. However, most outfitters transport their clients on horses, which usually means they'll be concentrating their efforts near the trails or other rideable locations. Get away from these places to find the best chance of tagging an older bull, whether you hunt the archery season with a bow or scour the mountains later with a rifle.

The Garnet Range receives much hunting pressure and has low bull-to-cow ratios in most places. Most of the bull harvest occurs in the first week of the season. Unless you're firmly committed to shooting a bull, the Garnets are an ideal place to draw an antlerless tag. Drawing odds are best in the eastern portion of the range (HD 291), but public access is more difficult.

Unless you plan to hunt close to a vehicle, the best hunting advice for the John Long Mountains is simple—get in shape. West of Sandstone Ridge in the large roadless areas, the terrain is very demanding. However, persistent backcountry hunters have a reasonable chance of taking a big bull. Competent archery hunters also do very well in these mountains, as September weather is conducive to backcountry camping and travel, and the vocalizations of bugling bulls make them easier to find.

19

BOB MARSHALL
WILDERNESS COMPLEX

------------◆------------

Geographical Overview

The Bob Marshall Wilderness, including the Great Bear and Scapegoat areas, totals 1.5 million acres of roadless, unspoiled territory protected from development in 1940 by the U.S. Secretary of Agriculture. Surrounding the official wilderness are hundreds of thousands of acres of roadless lands and primitive areas, creating a colossal expanse of wild territory.

The scope of the Bob Marshall Wilderness itself is overwhelming. From east to west its typical span measures around sixty miles. From north to south along its eastern edge, 160 miles cover its boundary. Many roads and highways ring the wilderness, but not a single route crosses it in any direction. Nonetheless, backcountry travel via a web of well-established trails places nearly any destination with a few miles of a maintained footpath. However, reaching the interior of the "Bob" is challenging from any direction. Wilderness outfitters routinely pack their camps and hunters over twenty miles to their hunting grounds.

Geographically, this region consists of several mountain ranges that lie on a northwest-southeast bearing. The Mission Mountains rise majestically from the west side of the Swan River valley, opposite the Swan Range, which looms to the east. The Flathead Range creates a northern finger of the Wilderness; the eastern portion is dominated by the Rocky Mountain Front. Mountains aren't particularly high in this region. Very few summits reach more than nine thousand feet.

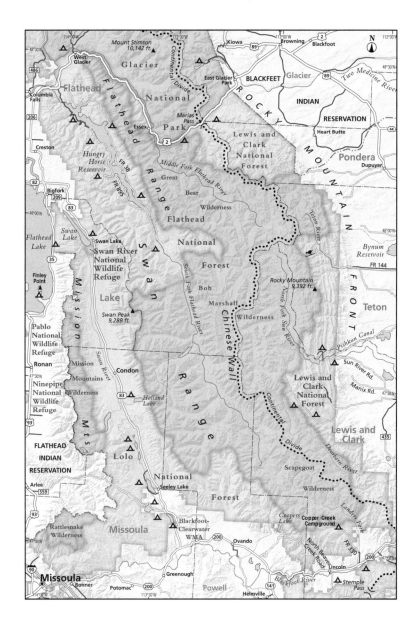

However, they are dishearteningly steep in many places, jutting abruptly from lowlands thousands of feet below the peaks.

In the southeast part of this region, open slopes, broad meadows, and river valleys mingle with forested slopes and basins. To the northwest, the timber becomes heavier, with fewer open areas and much thicker vegetation.

The vast character of the Bob Marshall Wilderness makes elk hunting difficult—and an adventure to be remembered.

Elk Distribution

Given the scope of this area, discussing the details of elk whereabouts would require a chapter in itself. Rather than dwell on specifics, general wintering grounds and travel routes to them will be described. This information should be useful to general-season hunters, who may find elk on winter range or attempt to ambush them on migration or staging areas when nasty weather pushes them from the wilderness.

On the east side elk pour from the backcountry to the foothills and valleys along the Rocky Mountain Front. These movements see animals weathering the cold months toward the upper ends of Dupuyer and Muddy creeks south of the Blackfoot Indian Reservation, and the Dearborn, Sun, and Teton rivers west of U.S. Highways 287 and 89. Many elk that winter in the Dearborn River drainage spend the summer and fall on the opposite side of the Continental Divide in the upper reaches of the Landers and North forks of the Blackfoot River. Autumn migrations take the herds down the Landers Fork and Alice Creek, then across the divide to the Dearborn country. Elk that winter in the Sun and Teton rivers are found west in the summer and fall, over the Continental Divide along the higher portions of the Spotted Bear River and the Middle Fork of the Flathead River.

Another major wintering area is found along the Blackfoot and Clearwater rivers in the lowlands around the confluence of these two streams and higher on the Blackfoot. The refuge provided by the Blackfoot-Clearwater Wildlife Management Area and surrounding area pulls elk from the southwest portion of the Bob Marshall Wilderness along the upper reaches of the South Fork of the Flathead River. Elk from the southern portion of the Mission Mountains descend to this area as well.

To the north, wapiti from the Swan Range east of Swan Lake drift into the bottoms along the South Fork of the Flathead River south of Hungry Horse Reservoir. Here they're joined by herds that move out of the Bob Marshall Wilderness from higher up the South Fork and others that trek over the mountains from the Flathead's Middle Fork. Many elk that lounge the high country of the Flathead Range east of Hungry Horse Reservoir in the summer drop to lower areas near the lake during the winter. Although heavy concentrations of elk use these major wintering grounds, smaller local populations are found elsewhere, some of which stay at lower elevations all year.

Where to Hunt

Hunting elk in the Bob Marshall Wilderness is a lifelong ambition for many resident hunters, but in the absence of livestock to pack your gear, the logistics of a wilderness hunt are very difficult. Hike-in hunting is possible in some places and can be very productive if you happen into elk moving from the interior of the various mountain ranges to their wintering areas. However, unless you have access to horses or mules to ride and pack, hiring the services of an outfitter is the way to go. But even if you do, maintain realistic expectations. Hunting the Bob is more about the wilderness experience than killing an elk. The clients of outfitters do drop some heavy-beamed old bulls each season, but success rates are typically low.

Three hunting districts in the interior of the wilderness (HDs 280, 150, and 151) open to general (rifle) elk hunting on September 15. Along with a portion of the Absaroka-Beartooth Wilderness, these are the only districts in the state where bull elk can normally be hunted during the rut with a rifle.

Dozens of trails lead from the perimeter into the wilderness. On the southwest side the trails that spring from Holland Lake (take FR 44 east of State Highway 83 about seven miles south of Condon) are popular entry points. Trails 35, 110, and 120 offer access to the Gordon Creek and Big Salmon Creek drainages, which flow east into the South Fork of the Flathead River.

From the south, FR 330 heads north of State Highway 200 about six miles east of Lincoln. Some eight miles from the highway, you'll find Copper Creek Campground and a trailhead. Trail 481, which heads up the North Fork of Copper Creek, and trail 438, which runs east for a couple of miles then swings northwest along the Landers Fork of the Blackfoot River, both originate at this trailhead.

Hunting on the east side of this region is confounded by the Sun River Game Preserve west of Choteau and Augusta. This area includes country east of the North Fork of the Sun River to the Continental Divide and is closed to hunting. For this reason, trails on the Teton River that skirt the north end of the preserve are favored by many hunters. To reach this area, take Canyon Road (FR 144), which launches west of Highway 89 about five miles north of Choteau along the Teton River. It's a little over twenty miles to the boundary of the Lewis and Clark National Forest. Trails branch from FR 144 at various intervals. Expect tough hunting and scattered elk in a gorgeous autumn setting.

On the north side of the Bob Marshall complex, access is possible from numerous areas south of Highway 2. Some of the best prospects are found in the Marias Pass area, where several trails head into the backcountry along the South Fork of Two Medicine River. FR 569 runs south of the highway about three miles west of the pass, offering a mix of hike-in and road-based hunting. West of this area, the terrain on the east side of the Flathead Range is very steep and not a particularly friendly place to hunters . . . or elk. However, trail 155, which heads up the Middle Fork of the Flathead River at Bear Creek trailhead about thirteen miles west of Marias Pass, winds into huntable country if you're willing to make the hike.

From the west, trails in the South Fork of the Flathead River drainage south of Hungry Horse Reservoir boast numerous routes into the wilderness. Two roads, FR 38 and FR 895, wind along opposite sides of the reservoir south of the sparse settlement of Hungry Horse. The lake spans about thirty miles as the boat floats, so expect a long drive to the South Fork's inlet. Another five miles or so beyond the inlet the routes converge near the Spotted Bear Campground. About two miles before the campground, FR 2826 continues up the river. From here the Meadow Creek trailhead sends several paths into the wilderness. Near the Spotted Bear Campground, FR 568 branches east along the Spotted Bear River, leading to four trailheads (South Creek, Trail Creek, Middle Big Bill and Silvertip) that boast no fewer than seven routes into the wilderness.

In addition to the popular trails described above, many other paths lead into the Bob. For hike-in or backpack hunting, some of the more remote trailheads are appealing. Expect less congestion and livestock at most of these, with the potential for shorter travel to huntable locations as well.

Although backcountry elk hunting sparkles as the highlight of this region, don't overlook other opportunities elsewhere. Elk can be found outside the Bob all fall, with numbers increasing substantially when wintry weather pushes animals from the high country. Many, many access roads lead to public lands in the Swan and Clearwater River valleys. Substantial road closures by Plum Creek Timber and the Forest Service in the mid-1990s greatly reduced hunting pressure in these areas. However, anyone with even a smidgen of ambition can find good hunting by hiking the gated roads.

Table 19-1 Bob Marshall Wilderness Complex

	Low	Moderate	High	Very High
Elk Numbers*	●			
Hunters Per Square Mile*	●			
Hunters Per Elk*		●		
Trophy Potential^	●			
Remote/Roadless Areas				●

* Elk numbers and hunting pressure may be much higher in certain areas as animals move to winter range.
^ Older bulls make up a notable percentage of the harvest, but hunter success rates are fairly low.

Hunting Strategies

Compared to many other parts of the state, elk numbers in the Bob Marshall Wilderness are fairly low. Unguided, new-to-the-area hunters should stay on the move and do lots of glassing to find animals. Bulls are vocal when the general season opens in September, but other hunters are, too. Unless you're quite skilled in distinguishing the sounds of the real thing from a well-blown imitation, just because you hear a bugle in the next drainage doesn't mean it's an elk.

Many folks pack two dozen miles into the wilderness to hunt, but that's not always necessary. A number of years ago, my boss, his wife, and I took three riding and two pack horses up a little-used trail, then struck out cross-country for a few miles. We camped "just" seven miles from the trailhead. No one killed a bull, but we got into elk and had a grand time. Ambitious backpackers could undertake a similar hunt.

No matter where or how you hunt the wilderness, don't forget that bears, black and grizzly, share the mountains. You must take food storage and other precautionary measures when you camp. Additionally, if you kill an elk and can't retrieve it to camp or a trailhead right away, do what you

Horses aren't absolutely necessary to hunt the Bob Marshall Wilderness, but if you kill a big Bob bull you'll wish you had some.

can to reduce the chances of a bear dining on your meat. If you quarter, bone, or cape the animal for packing, accomplish these tasks immediately. Stash the meat, cape, and antlers in a visible location well away from the gut pile and carcass. When you return, watch the area carefully before you approach to make sure a bear hasn't usurped your kill. If it has, report the situation to MDFWP personnel as quickly as possible.

Although wilderness hunting is the best this region offers in terms of an exhilarating experience, success rates are often better in nonwilderness settings later in the season as elk move to winter range. However, where wapiti experience significant hunting pressure on wintering grounds, they'll often stage at higher elevations prior to moving onto the lowlands—after the season closes. One example of this often occurs when elk from the Scapegoat Wilderness camp out near the Continental Divide before dropping to winter range along the Dearborn River. Muster the ambition to climb into staging areas above the foothills in late season, and you may find yourself blissfully alone among literally hundreds of elk.

20

PURCELL MOUNTAINS, SALISH MOUNTAINS, WHITEFISH RANGE

-------------◆-------------

Geographical Overview

The extreme northwestern corner of Montana is also its wettest. Annual rain and snowfall eclipse that found in elk country to the southeast, sprouting extremely heavy vegetation. Fast-growing deciduous trees such as aspen and alder, along with numerous species of evergreens dominate this region, where the primary land use is logging. Logged-over areas in various stages of regrowth checkerboard the landscape. Although some folks decry timber harvest in any form, these openings stimulate the production of grass, forbs, and shrubs, creating essential habitat for elk and other large mammals.

Although the mountains of this area aren't terribly high by Treasure State standards (few peaks top seven thousand feet), they can be quite steep. Western larch (tamarack) trees compose a considerable percentage of the forest cover. However, these "evergreens" aren't evergreen at all. Each autumn their needles turn fiery gold before dropping from the branches just like the leaves on nearby aspens. This fall phenomenon creates a beautiful mosaic of color that blesses those hearty souls who stalk elk with bow and arrow in the early days of October.

Elk Distribution

Elk numbers are very low throughout this region, to the extent that some may question the wisdom of even including these mountain ranges in a "where to go" book.

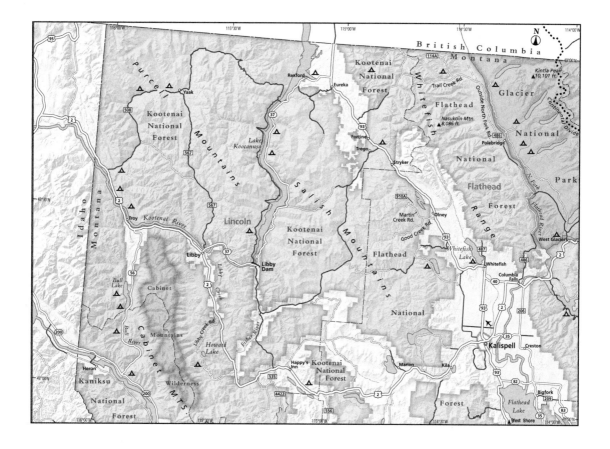

However, populations are increasing somewhat, with plenty of potential for further growth. The dry cycle that persists in the Northern Rockies may actually benefit this region's wapiti. Despite their short-term devastation, forest fires stimulate the production of the plants and trees the area needs to support more elk.

In the Purcell Mountains, elk winter in narrow river valleys, dispersing to higher elevations for the summer. Toward the south, animals drift into the south-facing slopes on the north side of the Kootenai River between Libby Dam and Libby, with others congregating around the Kootenai Falls area east of Troy. To the north, elk winter along the lower slopes adjacent to Lake Koocanusa.

Moving eastward, elk in the Salish Mountains favor the Thompson and Fisher River lowlands during the winter, ascending to higher country on their tributaries during the summer and fall. Wapiti also

The last rays of light kiss peaks in the Whitefish Range. These mountains aren't terribly high, but they are rugged.

congregate on the Dancing Prairie Preserve north of Eureka during the snowy months.

The valley along the North Fork of the Flathead River supports most of the wintering elk from the east side of the Whitefish Range. Concentrations are particularly high in the Home Ranch Bottoms vicinity west of Logging Creek. Good numbers of elk also use the Woods Ranch WMA on the Canadian border east of Lake Koocanusa.

Where to Hunt

To put elk hunting in this region in perspective, consider that annual hunter-success rates routinely drop below 5 percent. Many of the elk that pass through area check stations are brought by opportunistic deer hunters who tuck an elk tag in their shirt pocket when they hit the mountains in pursuit of a backwoods whitetail. Unless you live in the area and have time to become intimately familiar with elk use in your

Table 20-1 Purcell, Salish, Whitefish Mountains

	Low	Moderate	High	Very High
Elk Numbers	•			
Hunters Per Square Mile*	•			
Hunters Per Elk*	•			
Trophy Potential^	•			
Remote/Roadless Areas~	•			

* Higher when including deer hunters who incidentally kill elk.
^ Older bulls make up a relatively high percentage of the harvest, but hunter success rates are very low.
~ Moderate in the Whitefish Range.

backyard, your odds of successfully hunting this region are low. Consequently, it seems futile to make specific access recommendations, other than to note that easy entry to the Flathead and Kootenai National Forests abounds.

Hunting Strategies

This region commends itself to two types of trophy hunters: archers and those confident in tackling tough country with few elk in the late season. Bowhunters possess the distinct advantage of being afield when rutting bulls are bugling. This is extremely beneficial where you must find small herds of elk scattered over very large areas. Significant fire activity occurred in the mid-1990s and the first years of the current millennium. In dry years small blazes and conflagrations sear the timber in local areas. These spots are monitored by Forest Service personnel and definitely worth exploring. A call to one of the national forest's district offices will help you pinpoint rejuvenating burns. Generally, it takes a few years after the fire for vegetation regrowth to occur on a scale that attracts elk.

The prospects of downing a big, late-season "snow bull" might also tempt gamblers to try this region. Pretty much every major drainage has at least one road open to vehicles, with lots of gated routes open to exploration on foot. When snow hits, cruise the roads in your pickup until you cut elk tracks, preferably a single set of outsize hooves. Hit the trail,

Though few in number, the bugling of bulls in this region aids in their location—a definite advantage for bowhunters.

and pray you don't bump the bull into a deer hunter sitting on a stump in the next drainage. Drop an old stag under these conditions, and you've truly killed the bull of a lifetime, no matter how it measures to the "official" scorekeepers.

21

CABINET, COEUR D'ALENE MOUNTAINS

----------◆----------

Geographical Overview

Southwest of Libby, the Cabinet Mountains are a wild, beautiful expanse seen by few of the tourists that flock to Montana each summer. Although the peaks of this range generally measure sixty-five hundred to seventy-five hundred feet above sea level, the mountains rise from some of the lowest terrain in the state, giving them elevation gains from base to summit that rival more lofty peaks in the southwest.

At eighty miles long from north to south, the Cabinets represent a considerable barrier to east-moving storms that sweep inland from the Pacific. Moisture-laden air from the coast drops heavy precipitation on these mountains, producing dense stands of evergreens, including beautiful cedars that flank many of the creeks.

Much of the east side of the mountains is dominated by narrow, east-west creek bottoms flanked by steep slopes. Although the west side also sports daunting territory, its topography includes areas of more easily traversed terrain. The southeastern portion of the range consists primarily of lower peaks flanked by friendlier slopes.

Toward the center of the range, the Cabinet Mountain Wilderness claims the highest and most rugged country. Outside the hundred thousand acres of designated wilderness lie several other expansive tracts of roadless country, making the Cabinets an attractive destination for folks who cherish solitude.

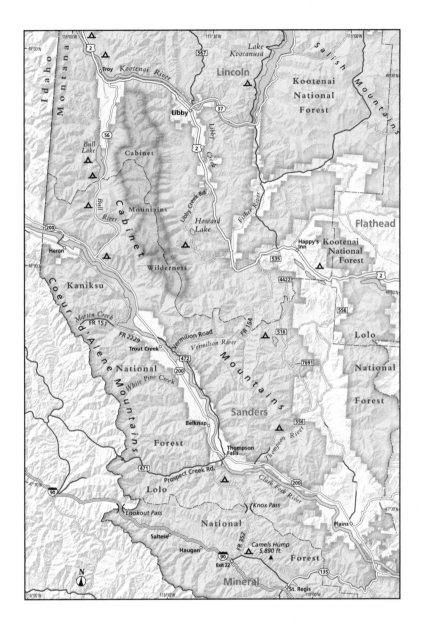

On the Montana-Idaho line southwest of the Cabinet Mountains, the Coeur d'Alene Mountains are essentially a northern spur of the Bitterroots. Geographically, this range is somewhat similar to the Cabinets, but with slightly lower summits. As you travel from north to south in the Coeur d'Alene Range, the country becomes increasingly steep, especially in the area just north of St. Regis.

The mountains in this region receive abundant precipitation. If you hunt here, expect some snow.

Elk Distribution

Rapid timber growth and fire suppression couple to keep most of this region well forested, which provides good escape cover for elk but produces generally poor winter range. Exceptions to this trend usually occur along major river bottoms and south-facing hillsides adjacent to the streams. Elk congregate in these places when the snow flies, but the quality of winter range in this entire area is severely threatened by the proliferation of invasive weeds, which are often spread to new areas by vehicles—pickups and ATVs piloted by hunters can easily become culprits.

Nonetheless, elk numbers are higher in this region than to the north. The Thompson, Clark Fork, and St. Regis River valleys are major wintering grounds. However, wapiti spread throughout the mountains in the summer and fall to the extent that a major analysis of elk distribution by the MDFWP indicates that animals are found in all drainages in these mountains at some season.

Heavy timber grows on the slopes of the Cabinet Mountains. The cover makes for tough hunting, but bulls grow big.

Where to Hunt

The vast majority of land in this region consists of national forest, with some state and PCT tracts also present in places. Public access for elk hunting is excellent, with numerous options available for close-to-the-road or backcountry settings. Permanent or seasonal closures occur on many roads shown on larger national forest maps, so it's wise to secure information and travel maps from the Kootenai National Forest Office in Libby as you plan your hunt.

Cabinet Mountains

Northwest of Heron, the Montana-Idaho border departs its rambling route along the crest of the mountains to shoot straight north to the Canadian line. East of this border, a considerable block of territory falls between the state line and State Highway 56, which runs along Lake Creek and the Bull River. Several sizeable blocks of roadless land lie in this area, offering good prospects for semi-remote hunting from several roads.

Two routes into this vicinity depart from near Troy on U.S. Highway 2. Just south of Troy, FR 427 heads west up Callahan Creek. About six miles from the highway, FR 424 forks south into the South Callahan Creek drainage, while FR 427 continues west. Not far beyond the fork in the road (some three miles) lies Idaho, but hunting in fairly remote country is possible to the north and south along the border. About two miles south of Troy, FR 384 departs Highway 2 south along Lake Creek. About seven miles in, FR 473 runs west into the Keeler Creek drainage. It's around thirteen miles to the Idaho line, with roadless territory on either side of the route.

Numerous trailheads ring the Cabinet Mountain Wilderness, yielding access from every side. From the west several options are available southeast of Bull Lake via two easy-to-find roads. Roughly nine miles north of State Highway 200, FR 407 launches east of Highway 56 just after it crosses the Bull River. About eight miles from the highway, trail 646 heads up the East Fork of the Bull River into the wilderness. Further on (about three miles) trail 966 makes a breathtaking ascent to Dad Peak. Some two miles south of Bull Lake, FR 410 heads east of Highway 56. A two-mile drive leads to FR 2722 and trails 978 and 972 that follow the Middle and North Forks of the Bull River. Look for elk on high ridges and in secluded basins during archery season or toward the beginning of the general season when there's little or no snow for animals to contend with in the high country.

At least ten trails reach the east side of the Cabinet Mountain Wilderness. However, many of these whisk up narrow creek bottoms separated by sharp ridges in country inhospitable to travel by humans or elk. Friendlier terrain to wapiti and hunters is often found outside the wilderness boundary in roadless areas at lower elevations. Don't overlook these while rushing to the sanctuary of designated wilderness.

To the north, the Flower Creek drainage covers a sizeable section of country in and outside the Cabinet Mountain Wilderness. About one mile south of Libby on Highway 2, watch for access to Flower Lake Road (FR 128). Roughly eight miles from the highway, FR 128 reaches a trailhead. Trail 137 winds along Flower Creek into the wilderness, while trail 14 runs up the drainage divide between Flower Creek and Parmenter Creek. South of the trailhead lies another considerable block of roadless territory.

Similar access and terrain await the intrepid elk hunter further south in the Howard Lake area. Approximately thirteen miles south of Libby on Highway 2, Libby Creek Road (FR 231) winds some twelve miles up the creek before reaching Howard Lake. About two miles before the lake, FR 2316 leads to trail 119, which heads into the wilderness. Near the lake, trail 117 heads south toward Standard Creek. From Howard Lake, FR 231 continues south, crossing a divide before dropping into Standard Creek and West Fisher Creek before it reconnects with Highway 2 near the confluence of West Fisher Creek and the Fisher River.

South of the Cabinet Mountain Wilderness, a notable block of semi-remote country with gentler contours is located in the Vermillion River drainage. To reach this area, aim for Vermillion Road, found east of Highway 200 just north of its crossing the Noxon Reservoir a mile or so

Table 21-1 Cabinet Mountains

	Low	Moderate	High	Very High
Elk Numbers*		●		
Hunters Per Square Mile^	●			
Hunters Per Elk^	●			
Trophy Potential~	●			
Remote/Roadless Areas			●	

* Numbers tend to increase toward the south.
^ Higher when including deer hunters who incidentally harvest elk.
~ Older bulls make up a significant portion of the harvest, but hunter success rates are generally low.

north of Trout Creek. About four miles south on Vermillion Road, FR 154 heads east along the Vermillion River, winding over twenty-five miles into the mountains. Numerous trailheads are found along this route, offering hike-in access to the Vermillion River-Silver Butte Creek divide and isolated drainages south of the river. Target the high ridges and elevated basins in this area early in the fall before wintry conditions push elk to lower elevations.

Coeur d'Alene Mountains

Montana's side of the Coeur d'Alene Mountains lies in a ribbon between the Idaho border and the Clark Fork River. This strip spans around twenty miles in the south from east to west, narrowing to around ten miles in the north. From north to south, the range covers approximately seventy miles.

Unless you want to start in Idaho, Highway 200 represents the primary access corridor into this area, with a few routes also launching north of I-90. Roads head west of Highway 200 into most major drainages, with more remote territory commonly occurring along the ridges in between creek bottoms. Overall, road densities are considerably higher toward the south, although permanent and seasonal closures limit vehicle travel in places.

Beginning at exit 22 on I-90, Twelvemile Road (FR 352) launches up Twelvemile Creek, crosses the divide near Knox Pass, then descends along Dry Creek to Thompson Falls on Highway 200. This route extends in excess of thirty miles, with numerous branch routes offering additional access into the rugged Camel's Hump area to the east and trails west of Knox Pass. It's fairly tough hiking from the road in places, but hunters who put some space between themselves and this well-traveled route find good prospects for locating elk.

West of Thompson Falls, State Highway 471 (FR 7 or Prospect Creek Road) follows Prospect Creek, reaching the Idaho border some twenty miles later at Thompson Pass. Many spur routes branch from this highway, some with travel restrictions that vary from archery to the general elk season. Given these limitations, a good mix of hike-in and vehicle-based hunting is found in this area, depending on your preferred style.

Table 21-2 Couer d'Alene Mountains

	Low	Moderate	High	Very High
Elk Numbers		•		
Hunters Per Square Mile		•		
Hunters Per Elk		•		
Trophy Potential	•			
Remote/Roadless Areas		•		

Roughly seventeen miles north of Thompson Falls, FR 215 heads west along White Pine Creek for about twelve miles before winding steeply up the north side of the drainage, where it reaches trail 761. After a short hike, this trail connects to trail 763, which runs along the White Pine Creek–Trout Creek divide. Hunting is possible along this ridge, or check out remote basins in this area near the Montana-Idaho divide. A sizeable parcel of roadless land covers the upper portion of Trout Creek, which can also be accessed via trail 774 at the end of FR 214 west of Highway 200 at Trout Creek.

North of Trout Creek on the west side of the Noxon Reservoir, another primary access route into Coeur d'Alene country awaits at Marten Creek. From Trout Creek, watch for FR 2229, which follows the west shore of the reservoir to Marten Creek Campground on Marten Creek Bay. Into Marten Creek Bay gurgles—you guessed it—Marten Creek. FR 151 winds west up Marten Creek. About seven miles from the campground, this route branches into several spur routes a few miles shy of the Idaho border.

Hunting Strategies

Preparing for adverse weather is an important factor when strategizing to hunt this region. Abundant precipitation often occurs during the archery and general elk seasons, when steady rain soaks undergrowth, slicks walking surfaces, and takes a toll on hunters and their equipment. Late-season hunters often greet heavy, wet snow, which greatly increases the effort required to traverse the mountains. Keeping yourself and your gear dry may be a real challenge.

With its heavy cover and dispersed elk, competent bowhunters looking for a big bull in a backcountry setting should definitely consider this region. Skill with a bugle and cow call are definitely advantageous for archers, as locating bulls via sound is as important as discovering them with sight. Animals are often found at high elevations (ridgetops and hanging valleys) early in the fall. With this in mind, many experienced arrow-slingers begin their hunts high, then drop lower if they don't find elk.

General-season hunters can also benefit from the bugle. In many places bulls will rip out a bugle of their own on opening morning of the season or answer the bugle of a hunter. Bulls in areas of low hunting pressure may respond to a bugle even later. Dusk and dawn are the most likely times to elicit a response. Even if you don't bugle yourself, keep your ears open for bulls feeling the urge to cut loose with a post-rut roar.

I generally steer clear of road-hunting from a pickup or ATV, but after a fresh snow, driving backroads in this area until you cross elk tracks is a worthwhile tactic. Once it's found, you'll need to follow the trail on foot. Tracking is probably my favorite way to hunt elk, yielding intense moments of excitement when you spot your quarry and severe seasons of disappointment when they spot you. Once on a trail, pay close attention when the tracks begin to meander or you notice signs that the elk have slowed to feed. In most cases, you're probably within two hundred yards of the herd.

22

NORTHERN BITTERROOT MOUNTAINS, NINEMILE VALLEY

------------◆------------

Geographical Overview

North of Lolo Pass, the character of the Bitterroot Range begins to change from that further south. Mountain summits aren't quite as high, nor do they possess the jagged, stony character of their southern kinfolk. Precipitation increases, producing dense undergrowth in the creek bottoms, including occasional groves of water-loving cedars.

Toward the crest of the range, though, much of the country in the central portion of the northern Bitterroots is notably barren of timber, an emerald islet of lush, tundralike vegetation elegantly situated above the sea of dark timber below. Crystalline lakes grace numerous basins just below the Montana-Idaho divide, with countless tiny streams trickling from under snowbanks or springing from the mountainsides.

This area, known as the Great Burn, was created by a massive fire event in 1910 that scorched a quarter-million acres along the Bitterroot divide in Montana and Idaho. Lodgepoles pines sprouted after the conflagration, but many of these burned in subsequent fires before reproducing, leaving large areas free of coniferous trees. In their absence, the grasses, forbs, and wildflowers of alpine tundra proliferated, creating a wonderful stretch of country that my brother-in-law once described as a "miniature Glacier Park."

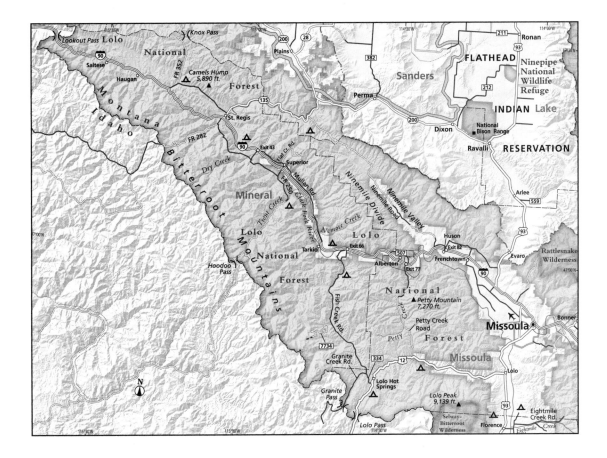

The largest roadless area in the United States lacking permanent protection as a designated wilderness, the Great Burn Roadless Area extends from Granite Pass, a few miles northwest of Lolo Pass on U.S. Highway 12 southwest of Missoula, to Hoodoo Pass, at the headwaters of Trout Creek south of Superior. From the top of the divide in the Great Burn on a clear day, the peaks of the Mission Mountains seem but a jaunt to the northeast, though a soaring eagle would wing sixty miles to reach them.

Opposite the Bitterroot Range, a series of mountains rises on the north side of the Clark Fork River. Ninemile Creek, which flows into the Clark Fork west of Frenchtown, drains the north side of this small mountain chain, while streams on the south side flow directly into the river. It has no formal title, but area residents often refer to this stretch of mountains as the "Ninemile Divide." Though lacking the breadth of the

Cliff Lake sits just below the Bitteroot Divide at the headwaters of Torino Creek. Timber grows quickly on the steep slopes, giving elk plenty of places to hide.

Bitterroots, several peaks along the Ninemile Divide rise to seven thousand feet, with steep terrain to match. In general, slopes on the north side of the divide, which extend from the Ninemile Creek valley, aren't as rugged as those to the south.

Elk Distribution

The prevalent pattern of elk distribution in western Montana applies almost perfectly to this region. Animals pass the summer and fall months at higher elevations in the mountains, then winter in the lowlands along stream corridors. Although larger herds concentrate in fairly specific locations toward the end of autumn, smaller bands are scattered in possibly every major drainage at the beginning of archery season in early September.

Elk herds winter in the Ninemile Creek valley, particularly on the lower end, where some animals remain year-round. On the south side of the Ninemile Divide, considerable numbers move into the Nemote Creek area north of Tarkio, but animals are also distributed farther west on the south-facing slopes above the Clark Fork River. Scattered herds range on the north side of the Ninemile Creek valley to the divide between Ninemile Creek and the Clark Fork and Jocko rivers.

South of the Clark Fork River, from Lolo Creek all the way to the headwaters of the St. Regis River near Lookout Pass, wapiti favor the lower portions of major creek drainages during the winter. From these areas they track back into the high country of the Bitterroot Mountains, with many populating the shady vales just under the Montana-Idaho divide. Lolo, Petty, Fish, Trout, Cedar, Dry, and Little Joe creeks (listed from east to west) number among the major stream corridors, though elk winter (and summer) in numerous other areas as well. Traditionally, overall elk numbers have been high in the Fish Creek–Lolo Creek drainages northwest of

A herd of elk grazes a meadow not far from Ninemile Creek. September snow dusts Squaw Peak, a dominate landmark in the area.

Highway 12. However, wolf activity has increased dramatically in the Fish Creek area in recent years, leading some observers to believe that elk reproduction has suffered accordingly.

Where to Hunt

Access to the Ninemile Divide and portions of the Lolo National Forest north of the Ninemile Creek valley is easily gained from Ninemile Road (FR 412), which idles along its namesake creek. To reach it, take State Highway 507 from exit 82 on the north side of I-90. Follow the highway west about two miles to Ninemile Road.

For the first fifteen miles or so, Ninemile Road passes through private land. It then reaches the national forest, although a narrow strip of private land alternates with public in places. At intervals along this route, access roads lead north and south to the national forest. In most cases these primary roads branch profusely with more primitive routes, many of which are closed to vehicles during the archery and general elk seasons. Take your pick. Drive the open roads, or opt for easy hiking away from your vehicle on the gated routes.

Several major access corridors wind into the steep, southern side of the Ninemile Divide, most of them springing from Mullan Road East on the north side of I-90 between Tarkio (exit 61) and Superior (exit 47). Beginning at exit 61, then working west, Nemote Creek Road (FR 454) is located about one mile down the road. Approximately seven miles farther, Second Creek Road (FR 283) launches at Lozeau. Some two miles east of Superior, Johnson Creek Road (FR 540) heads north into the mountains; Flat Creek Road (FR 194) is found just north of town. West of Superior on Mullan Road West, still on the north side of I-90, Pardee Creek Road (FR 97) is located about four miles from town. A drive of another three or so miles yields access to Sloway Gulch Road (FR 389). Each of these routes leads to multiple spur roads higher in the mountains, governed by various travel restrictions. Expect the best hunting in places where you can get a mile or more from direct vehicle access. But road hunters do get lucky. While living on a ranch near Huson, I heard of a local kid from Superior who dropped a big six-point bull within shouting distance of his pickup.

Table 22-1 Ninemile Valley Area

	Low	Moderate	High	Very High
Elk Numbers		●		
Hunters Per Square Mile		●		
Hunters Per Elk			●	
Trophy Potential	●			
Remote/Roadless Areas		●		

In the northern Bitterroot Mountains, elk hunters have it all, at least when it comes to access options. Want to drive the roads? Numerous lengthy routes run from I-90 to the Idaho divide. Looking for hike-in hunting with easy walking? Gated logging roads abound. Hankering for a backcountry adventure in unspoiled country? Tens of thousands of acres await in the roadless area of the Great Burn.

To the south, Petty Creek Road (FR 489) provides a major access corridor between I-90 and Highway 12. From exit 77 on I-90, this route heads south, traveling nearly twenty miles over the mountains to Highway 12. East of the road, a nice chunk of roadless country is found around Petty Mountain. About four miles south of the interstate, trail 773 climbs steeply to the Petty Creek–Albert Creek divide. Some seven miles further up the road, trail 718 departs from FR 5553. Elsewhere, numerous gated and open routes provide additional options for hunting.

Further west, Fish Creek Road (FR 343) runs south of exit 66 on I-90, traveling around thirty miles before reaching Highway 12 roughly seven miles north of Lolo Pass. The Fish Creek drainage has a reputation for good elk hunting, with many closed logging roads lower down, and access to several roadless areas higher up. About ten miles from I-90, FR 7750 veers west along Fish Creek, while FR 343 continues up the South Fork of Fish Creek and on to Highway 12. About seven miles from FR 343, FR 7750 reaches the Clearwater Crossing Campground. This is perhaps the most centrally located access point into Montana's portion of the Great Burn Roadless Area. Trail 101 heads south up the West Fork of Fish Creek, with several branch trails stemming from this path. Trail 103 launches north along the North Fork of Fish Creek, while trail 99 winds west along Straight Creek.

Some five miles north of the Fish Creek–Lolo Creek divide, two roadless areas are located in the Cache Creek and Burdette Creek drainages. On the north side of FR 343, watch for trail 2 at Grovedale. This path follows Burdette Creek into roadless territory that spans some twenty-three square miles. About two miles north, FR 4218 begins on the south side of FR 343. A mile's drive leads to the Cache trailhead and trail 317, which follows Cache Creek into a roadless area of over thirty-five square miles. In all portions of the Fish Creek drainage, expect fine hunting at high elevations during archery season and the first part of the general season. Normal years find elk moving lower after snows deepen on the mountaintops in mid-November. However, in dry seasons elk may hang in lofty locales much longer.

Near the town of Superior, several major roads lead into the Bitterroot Mountains. Each is reached from the frontage road that parallels the south side of I-90. To find them, turn south from the interstate at exit 47. Hang a left (east) on the frontage road, then continue a little over a mile to Cedar Creek Road (FR 320) or continue another three miles to Trout Creek Road (FR 250). Each of these roads winds a twenty-odd mile course through the mountains to the top of the Montana-Idaho divide, with various branches, both gated and open to vehicles, leading to more isolated areas. Further west, Dry Creek Road (FR 342) charts a similar course to the divide from I-90 at exit 43.

Table 22-2 Northern Bitterroot Mountains

	Low	Moderate	High	Very High
Elk Numbers		●		
Hunters Per Square Mile		●		
Hunters Per Elk		●		
Trophy Potential		●		
Remote/Roadless Areas			●	

South of this route, a notable roadless region occurs in the rugged country spanning the Dry Creek–Thompson Creek divide. Trail 152 heads into this area about three miles from the interstate, but an easier route into the upper portion is found about seven miles farther in at trail 151. Few spur roads set out from FR 342, probably due to the wickedly steep terrain it follows.

From St. Regis west to the Idaho border at Lookout Pass on I-90, numerous access roads whisk right into the Lolo National Forest. Pretty much anywhere you find an exit on the interstate, you'll find an access point for vehicle entry into elk habitat. These major routes, and the contortion of logging roads that spring from them, appear on the map as contorted as a mass of earthworms in the bottom of a bait can. However, enough of these carry travel restrictions during the fall to spawn good hike-in hunting.

Hunting Strategies

Although the mountaintops of this region are a full two thousand feet lower than their brethren in the state's highest ranges, much of the country is extremely canted and difficult to hike. In addition to their steepness, many slopes are covered in deciduous underbrush, further thwarting casual entry by people.

In such spots you can usually narrow the best places to find elk by paying close attention to topography. I sometimes read articles advising hunters to look for elk, especially bulls, "on the nastiest slopes you can find." This advice confuses the exception with the rule. Elk, most notably wary, lone bulls, it is true, hole up in some ungodly locations when pressured by humans. However, I'm thoroughly convinced that wapiti don't enjoy plowing through brush or balancing their bulk on a precipitous sidehill any more than people.

With this characteristic in mind, it's possible to make hunting in tough country more efficient. Rather than tackling the inclines that wear one out in short order, look for benches, basins, and ridgetops, where it's easier for you (and elk) to travel. In one location I hunt, a narrow bench runs above a precipitous slope to the creek below. Animals travel through the steep part, but they bed and browse on the bench. On several occasions I've found bulls napping right on the edge, where they can quickly drop out of sight if disturbed.

Additionally, take advantage of the hundreds of miles of closed roads in this region. They make it much easier to travel and also facilitate retrieval should you drop your elk a couple of miles from a route open to vehicles. Quartered or boned, it's not much of a job to transport an elk on a game cart when there's a graded road to follow. If there's snow, you can cover the ground in a hurry when hiking gated roads, looking for tracks. Once they're found, take up the trail. Additionally, more than a couple of inches of snow makes it possible to transport meat on a plastic sled, a remarkably efficient and inexpensive way to get your elk from the woods to the back of the pickup.

ABOUT THE AUTHOR

------------◆------------

A third-generation Montana native of homesteader's stock, Jack Ballard grew up on a ranch west of Three Forks, hunting mule deer, antelope, and elk. Since then, he's logged over thirty years and countless miles in pursuit of elk.

In 1992 his first published photo appeared in the Rocky Mountain Elk Foundation's fledgling *Bugle Magazine*. The next year, *Rocky Mountain Game & Fish Magazine* carried his first written article. Since that time, Jack's articles have appeared in over thirty different regional and national magazines, including *American Hunter*, *Petersen's Hunting Magazine*, *Sports Afield*, *Colorado Outdoors*, *Deer & Deer Hunting*, *Montana Magazine*, and many others. His photos have graced the pages of numerous books (from the Smithsonian Press, Heinemann Library, and others), calendars, and magazines. Jack has received multiple awards for his writing and photography from the Outdoor Writers Association of America and other professional organizations.

While developing his writing career, Jack lectured in philosophy, religion, ethics, and education at Montana State University—Billings but now writes full time. He holds two master's degrees and is an accomplished public speaker, entertaining students, conference attendees, and recreation/conservation groups with his compelling narratives.

In addition to Western big-game hunting, Jack also writes about fishing, camping, canoeing, cross-country skiing, wildlife, and conservation. When not wandering the backcountry, he hangs his hat (temporarily) in Billings, Montana.

Ballard's first book, *Creating a Traditional Elk Camp: Where the Heart of the Hunt Is Found*, has received excellent reviews from writers and hunters across the nation. To see more of Jack's work, visit his Web site: www.jackballard.com.

INDEX

------------◆------------

Anaconda Mountains
state lands, 17
still-hunting, 9–10
Sweetgrass Hills. *See also* western
Missouri Breaks, Judith
Mountains, Sweetgrass Hills

T
Tendoy Mountains, 135–36. *See also*
Beaverhead, Tendoy, Pioneer,
Fleecer Mountains
Tobacco Root, Highland
Mountains, 121–29
elk distribution, 123–24
geographical overview, 121–22
hunting strategies, 128–29
where to hunt, 124–28
Tobacco Root Mountains, 124–26.
See also Tobacco Root, High-
land Mountains
tracking, 11

W
western Missouri Breaks, Judith
Mountains, Sweetgrass Hills,
92–99
elk distribution, 94–95
geographical overview, 92–94
hunting strategies, 99
where to hunt, 96–99
Whitefish Range. *See also* Purcell
Mountains, Salish Mountains,
Whitefish Range
winter, staging for, 5–6

Y
Yellowstone River breaks. *See also*
Snowy Mountains, Bull
Mountains, Yellowstone River
breaks

ABOUT THE ROCKY MOUNTAIN ELK FOUNDATION

------------ ◆ ------------

Founded in 1984 and headquartered in Missoula, Montana, the Rocky Mountain Elk Foundation is a nonprofit organization dedicated to ensuring the future of elk, other wildlife and their habitat. The Elk Foundation and its partners have permanently protected or enhanced more than 5 million acres, a land area nearly twice as large as Yellowstone National Park—and opened to public access more than 500,000 acres previously closed to hunting, fishing, and other recreation. The Elk Foundation upholds the hunting tradition by protecting places where wild animals will continue to thrive and people will continue to hunt. We strongly support and encourage hunting practiced with respect for the individual animal, the species, and the land. We believe that honest hunting for free-ranging animals kindles vitality in the individual hunter, deepens appreciation of wildlife and wildlands, and strengthens society as a whole.

To help protect wild elk country or learn more about the Rocky Mountain Elk Foundation, visit www.elkfoundation.org or call 800-CALL-ELK.